HE CHOSE ME
Don't Judge Me

HE CHOSE ME
Don't Judge Me

Jennifer Clark

Rain Publishing, LLC
KNIGHTDALE, NORTH CAROLINA

Copyright © 2014 by **Jennifer Clark**

All rights reserved. No part of this publication may be reproduced, distributed or transmitted in any form or by any means, including photocopying, recording, or other electronic or mechanical methods, without the prior written permission of the publisher, except in the case of brief quotations embodied in critical reviews and certain other noncommercial uses permitted by copyright law. For permission requests, write to the publisher, addressed "Attention: Permissions Coordinator," at the address below.

Jennifer Clark/Rain Publishing, LLC
PO Box 702
Knightdale, NC 27545
www.rainpublishing.com

Cover Design by Rain Publishing, LLC

Edited by Sherrian N. Crumbley/Rain Publishing, LLC.

Scripture references are from The Holy Bible, King James Version

Ordering Information: Quantity sales. Special discounts are available on quantity purchases by corporations, associations, and others. For details, contact the "Special Sales Department" at the address above.

He Chose Me/ Jennifer Clark. -- 1st ed.
ISBN 978-0-9908453-5-5

Library of Congress Control Number: 2014955264

Testimonials

To be chosen by God is one of the most precious gifts that we could ever receive. In this book, Elect Lady Jennifer Clark has done a masterful job of explaining the many challenges that we sometimes must go through, and then gives us hope not to give up because God has a plan for our lives, and that is to bring us to our destiny.

I know that many lives will be touched and blessed as they read the pages of this book. She has so much love and compassion to give to others, because of what she has learned in her journey to be a chosen vessel for God.

May God heal, deliver and transform many lives through the writing of Elect Lady Jennifer Clark.

Pastor, Author Sheryl J. Harrison
Prayer & Compassion Healing Power Ministry
Sacramento, CA 95823

Jennifer Clark is an extraordinary woman who defies the odds when it comes to inner strength and determination. I've never known her to give up on a dream and this is what makes her an incredible lady. Jennifer is truly a work of art. She reminds me of a beautifully woven quilt, with each piece fitted together perfectly, to show a colorful and perfect design. She is full of life and has God at the center of everything that she does. This book is remarkable in the way it illuminates my wife's transparency to give others hope. From the very beginning of our marriage and ministry, I've watched Jennifer grow as a wife, mother and a leader of the women's ministry in our church.

Jennifer's story is one that will keep you on the edge of your seat as she reveals truths about her life and the way God turned things around for the better. Each chapter in her book teaches a lesson for life while revealing a past that was not very kind to her at times. But against hope she continued to believe that life's challenges only prepared her for God's promises. Her message is simple, "Just because you've been knocked down, doesn't mean you can't, each time, get back up." She encourages woman all over the world that victory is in their ability to be transparent while telling their story.

There is a special chapter in her book written primarily to Elect Ladies. In her final chapter, she talks candidly about her life as an Elect Lady in the church. Though Jennifer's story is an eye opening story for women who have been broken and forgotten, it is yet another lesson for life to women around the world that through patience, prayer and careful study of God's word, all things work together for good if we believe in the Lord.

This book is anointed to change lives. Many will be touched as they read this compelling story of a life chosen to bless others.

Dr. Walter A. Clark, Jr.
Founder, Global Outreach Ministries, Inc.
Columbia, SC

Dedication

This book is dedicated to my two beautiful daughters, Lexi and Livi, and to the many women around the world, whom God is raising up in the earth today, who are willing to give birth to their calling and gifts. May you find your God-given talent and pursue it with all of your heart. Let everything you do be full of God's heart and mind. May you exemplify boldness and perseverance in spite of any adversaries that may rise up against you. Know that everything you're going through will be for God's glory. Believe in yourself!

Acknowledgments

I would like to express my gratitude to the many people who supported the vision of this book.

First and foremost, I would like to thank God for allowing me to survive the pain and hardship so I am now able to share my story of His goodness and mercy.

To my husband, Walter, thank you for standing beside me throughout my career. You have been my rock, inspiration and motivation in pushing me to pursue my dreams and vision. Thank you for your support, encouragement and patience with writing this book.

I also would like to thank my wonderful children: Lexi and Livi, for always making me smile and for understanding that the time I spent away, working on my projects, was all for the birthing of God's vision. I hope that one day you can read this book and understand why I spent so much time in front of my computer.

To Pastors, Sheryl and Eddie Harrison, thank you for your continual support of the vision of our ministry and the birthing of this book.

To the publicists, editors, designer, and photographer, thank you for helping me to bring this vision to pass. Your hard work and dedication is greatly appreciated!

Special thanks to all my mentors, family, and friends for your encouragement to help me complete this book. I would have probably given up without your support and love.

CONTENTS

Introduction

CHAPTER ONE
You are Chosen 1

CHAPTER TWO
Don't Judge Me 17

CHAPTER THREE
Walking in Deliverance 37

CHAPTER FOUR
He Chose Me 47

CHAPTER FIVE
Pregnant with Possibilities 63

CHAPTER SIX
From the Pit to the Palace 75

CHAPTER SEVEN
You are Worthy 83

CHAPTER EIGHT
A Mother's Love 95

CHAPTER NINE
Keep Your Vision Alive 103

CHAPTER TEN
This is Your Season 119

CHAPTER ELEVEN
The Anointing 127

CHAPTER TWELVE
For Pastor's Wives Only 135

ABOUT THE AUTHOR 147

Introduction

By the grace of God, I was able to overcome the power of the enemy and so can you. The devil's plan for my life was interrupted by God's divine power.

The devil always has a hidden agenda. His number one goal is to destroy the people of God. Because our heavenly Father is the supreme God of the universe, Satan's scheme can be over powered at any time. God is omniscient. He knows all, He sees all. There is nothing you can hide from Him. He sees everything whether you're in the dark, in a cave, or under the ocean. He sees you.

Satan does have a great influence on some of the things that we see happening today. We read about killings, bombing, suicides, etc... Who is behind all of this evil? Satan. We have allowed him to come into our lives, our heart, and our mind to control us. God didn't give him the authority - we did. When we decided to turn our cheek against God, then we allowed Satan to be our God.

We are commanded to live by the Word of God. If you're not living by the law of God's word (Bible), then certainly you may be under the power and influence of Satan. I want to decree and declare to you this day that every wicked and evil power that may be ruling you now will one day be destroyed in the name of Jesus. You have the power to renounce every evil spirit that has entered into your family, your life, your ministry, and your health.

You have it in you! The Bible says that God has given us the power to escape the plans of the enemy. 1 Peter 1:3-11 says, "According as his divine power hath given unto us all things that pertain unto life and godliness, through the knowledge of him that hath called us to glory and virtue: Whereby are given unto us exceeding great and precious promises: that by these ye might be partakers of the divine nature, having escaped the corruption that is in the world through lust. And beside this, giving all diligence, add to your faith virtue; and to virtue knowledge; and to knowledge temperance; and to temperance patience; and to patience godliness; and to godliness brotherly kindness; and to brotherly kindness charity. For if these things be in you, and abound, they make you that ye shall neither be barren nor unfruitful in the knowledge of our Lord Jesus Christ. But he that lacketh these things is blind, and cannot see afar off, and hath forgotten that he was purged from his old sins. Wherefore the rather, brethren, give diligence to make your calling and election sure: for if ye do these things, ye shall never fall: For so an entrance shall be ministered unto you abundantly into the everlasting kingdom of our Lord and Savior Jesus Christ."

As you are reading this book right now, I want you to believe that you have the power to overcome every opposing force that is driving you to live an ungodly life. God has given you the power to defeat the enemy. All you have to do is believe in God's word and have faith that God will, not may, but will turn your situation around. Don't doubt yourself, don't doubt God but know that the Holy Spirit that lives inside of you is here, in your corner, to back you up. I'm here to tell you that "Yes, you can do it". Believe in yourself. Every day, when you wake up tell yourself, "Yes I can!" The Bible tells us that we can do all things with Jesus Christ.

If you believe in your heart that Jesus has died for your sins and He has forgiven you, then the only thing that God wants you to do now is walk in your victory.

Lord, I pray that your son or daughter who is reading this book right now will humble themselves under your authority. I pray that they will continue to trust and love you. We all have sinned and fallen short somewhere in our life time, but God, I am asking that you will forgive the individual of any wrong doing. Lord, redirect his or her path. Put things back in order. Anoint them for their destiny, their calling, and for the things you desire them to do. Lord, I pray that your child will reach and fulfill their purpose in the name of Jesus. I pray for their strength, faith, and walk with you. Amen.

CHAPTER ONE

You are Chosen

There is something greater on the inside of you in spite of what you see on the outside. As we read the Bible and study His word, we come across a few imperfect people. These were people who had a past, but God used them in spite of their imperfections. God saw fit to still use these individuals for His glory in spite of their flaws: Jacob was a fraudster; Peter had a bad temper; David was a murder; Noah was a drunk; Jonah hid from God; Paul killed innocent Christians; Gideon was rebellious; Miriam was a backbiter Martha was a busy-body; Mary Magdalene prostituted her body; Thomas was a doubter; Sarah was impatient; Moses stuttered his words; Zacchaeus was a short impostor.

When we look into the lives of these individuals, we see ourselves. They were like you and I today. We too have committed some of the same sins, but there is a God that will take imperfect people such as ourselves and turn each of us into a disciple, entrepreneur, a pastor, a missionary, a teacher or whomever He has called you to be. These people encouraged us throughout history. They let us know that God can see pass your past and into your destiny. Man may not see it but God sees the winner in you. Some of these people were low-down, dirty, unworthy, and unrighteous, but God saw greater. He saw the outcome of their future. He knew if He could get a "yes" in their heart, and a "yes" in their spirit, that He could turn the crooked path straight.

Sometimes in life we tell God who we want to be or what we desire to do. But as I can recall, it was He who made us. It was He who called us into existence. God knew who you were going to be before He called you into this world. He knew your purpose, He knew your destiny and He knew the plans for your life.

Many of us struggle today in life. We are confused about who we are, what we are called to do, or where we need to go on this journey. You may feel you are off course because of some setbacks, but God is a God who keeps His promise. Pray to God about your life and get on board. What are you waiting for? Your destiny lays waiting for you.

Your destiny is considered to be a predetermined course of events that you will experience once in this life. It is believed to be a path that all individuals will one day take to live out God's perfect will for their life.

In spite of our different paths in life, it is our responsibility to fulfill the journey that God has created for our lives. Staying on course can be a little complicated at times, as you know, due to sudden changes in our lives, unforeseen situations, or a lack of motivation. Not humbling ourselves to the voice of God can cause us to go astray when we make decisions based on what we want and not the desires of God. But in order for you to walk into your destiny, you must listen to the voice of God. Be led by the Holy Spirit for direction. When you wake up every morning, it is your duty to consult with God for your daily plan. Allow God to share with you His desired plans for your life. God wants us to be proactive in the earth. Your plan should never be the same from day to day. Life would be easier if we could do the same thing every day but after a while, life wouldn't be that interesting. Life is a journey. Having the direction of the Holy Spirit will allow you to walk into a divine path every day of your life.

In my walk, I've learned over the years that we often fail to notice the voice of God. Our lives and minds are so occupied with the everyday issues of life; we often miss the whispers of God. It is so important to seek Him as soon as you wake in the morning so you can know your route before you begin your day. Seeking Him in the midnight hour, or early in the morning, will allow you and God to communicate without distractions. Distractions come to mislead us at times. They occur to get you off course. You are now focusing on the things around you and not the things of God. When you are not focusing, you then allow the enemy to misguide you from your original plan of the day. God gives us a daily vision of how our day should go, but when you don't seek Him in the morning, you tend to put other things before God's original plan. When God gives you directions you must follow His lead at all times. Don't allow the enemy to get in your path of pursuing your destiny. Follow the voice of God.

You may wonder how you can hear from God. We hear voices all the time, so how do you know who you are listening to?

1. The voice of God/Holy Spirit
2. The voice of your ethics
3. The voice of reasoning/judgment
4. The voice of your flesh
5. The voice of others

6. The voice of Satan

With all of these voices, how can you determine which voice to follow? In John 16:13, Jesus says, "Howbeit when he, the Spirit of truth, is come, he will guide you into all truth: for he shall not speak of himself; but whatsoever he shall hear, that shall he speak: and he will shew you things to come."

At times, you may hear an audible voice; other times, you may experience a special feeling within your spirit or within your heart. God's voice may also come unprompted through thoughts, visions, and impressions. The Lord speaks to His children on a daily basis. It is through the Holy Spirit that He communicates to us. The Holy Spirit is the third person of the Trinity (co-equal with God the Father and God the Son). The Holy Spirit lives within every born-again believer.

John 14:15-17 says, *"If ye love me, keep my commandments. And I will pray the Father, and he shall give you another Comforter, that he may abide with you forever; Even the Spirit of truth; whom the world cannot receive, because it seeth him not, neither knoweth him: but ye know him; for he dwelleth with you, and shall be in you."*

It is important to have a relationship with the Lord. It is through your relationship with the

Lord that you will know and trust Him. We have a tendency to mistrust those that we don't know, but if you would develop a personal relationship with the Lord, you will allow Him to be the navigator of your life. There are times in our lives when we tend to lose focus due to unplanned events, circumstances, and road blocks. These events often occur due to poor judgment, bad decision making, or a lack of understanding. We often react before we think. It is extremely valuable to have a level head, or clear mind, so you can allow the Holy Spirit to operate freely in your life.

When your mind is not free or your thoughts are not pure, you often battle with the Lord. It causes our flesh to be in disagreement with the spirit of the Lord. Whether you realize it or not, when we come against the plans of God, we are walking in disobedience. Every decision we make must line up with the Word of God.

When you learn to listen to the voice of God, it is then your life will be lived out according to His will. We can listen to everything around us but God. Everything is keeping us so entertained these days: the different genres of music, explicit shows on television, demonic movies, and seductive garments, along with the everyday challenges of life. All of these things were designed to keep us bound in the mind, bound in the flesh, and bound in the spirit. It is important that you guard your spirit and mind from every evil thought and action. This world is full of the lust of flesh. The Bible commands us to walk into the newness of life and put the former things behind. We are to die daily to the impurities of the flesh.

What I like about God is that He has already predetermined the plan for our lives. No matter what has happened in your past, God still will allow you the opportunity to get back on board. We all have made bad decisions or taken an unplanned turn, but I am a living testimony that God is a God of a second chance. Man may give up on you, but we serve a God that is a forgiving God.

It was in the year 2002. I will never forget. I encountered a date with my destiny (spiritually thinking). The story goes something like this: I was getting out of my car at a grocery store. While getting my daughter out of the car, suddenly I heard a voice within say, "There's a gentleman that is about to approach you; don't be afraid." At that time I didn't understand, but I was being warned by the Holy Spirit about this male approaching me to keep me from being startled from his presence. So I turned around, looked for the man, and my eyes went directly on him as he was walking pass the grocery store. The voice on the inside said, "That's him." He was a young male, thinly built, wearing a hat and a jogging suit, and walking very swiftly like he was on an assignment. He then walked pass the grocery store and before I knew it, he approached my vehicle. He said, "Miss, Can I talk to you?" I replied, "Sure, what do you need?" He said, "I am a sent prophet by God." I was in shock a little, not knowing what a prophet was (I only heard of such term in the Bible), I was trying to picture in my mind how a prophet is supposed to look.

God sent the prophet to me on that day to speak a word of encouragement into my life. The Lord wanted me to know that He still had plans for my life in spite of my appalling mistakes. The young man proceeded to tell me the things of God. This prophet was definitely on an assignment. As I began to shop, he began to tell me things of God concerning my life and my daughter's future. The prophecies went on for at least 15 minutes or so, as I continued to shop. I went to the cash register to pay for my groceries; he was still prophesying. I walked to my car and put the groceries into my car; he still was prophesying. I am going to admit, I was a little embarrassed at the time because it was strange to walk around a grocery store listening to a man I never met before, talk about God's plan for my life.

As I finished packing the groceries into my car, he asked if he could finish speaking. Unfortunately, I had somewhere to go so I had to cut him off and I never saw him again. Words of wisdom: don't ever cut God short. Learn to rearrange your schedule because you might miss some important information or your miracle.

I often reflect back to the words that were given to me from God, through the prophet, on that day. The words he prophesied were the new beginnings of my life. God spoke words of encouragement to me that day. I was dealing with a lot of hurt during that time, but the Word of the Lord lifted me. The Lord spoke to me concerning His plans for my life. Trust me, His plans were bigger than I could have imagined. He told me who I was going to become and the things I would one day experience. I can truly say that everything that was said on that day has unfolded or has been repeated by another prophet or person in my life. On that day, because of the spoken prophetic words, I decided to follow Jesus even more.

After receiving the word of the Lord I went and told others. I was excited at first, but after sharing my testimony with others, my excitement turned into misery. People didn't believe me and said things like, "There's no prophet walking on earth" or "Those people are out to get your money". Talk about confused! I didn't know who to believe. I found myself questioning God. So I played the whole scenario back in my head: this total stranger walked up to me discussing the things of God and not once tried to get my number for a relationship, so why not believe that it was God? Everything felt so peaceful in my spirit concerning the gentlemen and the word. I finally stopped rationalizing in my mind and just believed that God paid me a special visit in the grocery store to let me know He had special plans for my life.

Not only did God visit me then, He is still with me now. After I met my husband years ago, I travelled with him to Sumter, S.C. to attend a Prophetic Revival, it was there I truly came into the presence of God Almighty. I believe God had a divine appointment waiting for me. It was there, in a small town where I met the presence of God. God used a well-known prophet to minister unto my spirit. During that time, my spirit was broken. I felt hurt, ashamed and disappointed due to the decisions I made in life.

God used this Man of God so mightily that night that I literally felt the heaviness (spirits) lifted from my body. I had a supernatural encounter that night. God encouraged me to keep going. He spoke greatness in my life. He told me I was going to have a brighter future than my past. That day was so special to me. I give God all the praise and honor. No one knew the inner struggles that I was facing. If God didn't speak to me that night, I probably would not have made it this far in life. But when the Lord said He had forgiven me and still had plans for my life, I was so grateful that He decided to give me another chance. God not only spoke to me through those vessels but also through other great leaders in the Body of Christ. I thank God for these leaders and ministers who have imparted wisdom into my life along the way. They have all helped me in some way: whether it was through words of encouragement or guidance throughout my life. I am very grateful to have come in contact with some great leaders in the ministry. They have assisted in the shaping of the woman I am today. One of my spiritual mentors has always encouraged me to go hard after God, no matter what happens in my life. I took that to heart and was able to move pass my failures in life to accomplish many of my dreams.

These events allowed me to see that God speaks to us in many ways. At times it may be an audible voice (Him), through our inner thoughts, feelings in our spirit, or through another human being. God is the same every day, but the way He comes to us may be different from day to day. It is so crucial that you develop a relationship with God so you can identify when God is speaking. When it seems like God is not listening, it is not that He can't hear us, but we don't hear Him. He is speaking to you now. He's trying to get your undivided attention concerning His plans for your life. If He can't get your attention, he often sends people into your life that will speak for Him. I thank God for those that He has used to speak a word into my life but I know it is also important for me to hear Him for myself.

My husband and I had often visited this church in West Columbia, S.C., from time to time. In a particular night service this church had a guest speaker whom we loved to hear speak. We didn't go just to hear a word from the Lord, but we love being in an atmosphere where you can feel the presence of God. On that night, the speaker asked what was taking us so long, meaning marriage. We were not dating that long; therefore, marriage was really not on our agenda because we both just came out of previous relationships. I think we were serious about our relationship, but not serious to marry within a few months. After that night, we began to take our relationship more seriously while allowing God to direct us in His plans for our lives. Soon after, we were married! We not only married each other because we loved each other but God used the woman of God to speak our marriage into existence.

I wasn't from an upscale neighborhood but God still saw something great in me. I wasn't living the best lifestyle, but God saw fit to minister to me to build me up. God has special plans for you as well. I don't care what walk of life you came from, your nationality, or your living conditions, God has a written-out plan for your life that He wants you to open and begin to step forward in it. It may not come through a prophet, a friend, or even your pastor. God may speak directly to you. All I know is that God wants you to be encouraged. He desires to have a conversation with you. However, with all the technology and worldly (secular) life-styles that the devil has made so convenient for us, we have become too occupied for God. Stop and listen for Him as He whispers to your spirit. Whatever you do, don't abort your destiny. God has plans for you!

CHAPTER ONE
Questions for Consideration

Is the Lord trying to get your attention?

What does your future look like?

What are some goals you want to accomplish in life?

Are you seeking the Lord for directions?

If God has spoken to you about some things that pertain to you, take the time to write them down and reflect upon your notes from time to time.

Scriptures of Reflection

Proverbs 3:5 - Trust in the LORD with all thine heart; and lean not unto thine own understanding.

Ephesians 2:8 - For by grace are ye saved through faith; and that not of yourselves: [it is] the gift of God...

2 Corinthians 5:7 - For we walk by faith, not by sight...

Hebrews 11:6 - But without faith [it is] impossible to please [him]: for he that cometh to God must believe that he is, and [that] he is a rewarder of them that diligently seek him.

1 John 5:4 - For whatsoever is born of God overcometh the world: and this is the victory that overcometh the world, [even] our faith.

Mark 9:23 - Jesus said unto him, If thou canst believe, all things [are] possible to him that believeth.

CHAPTER TWO

Don't Judge Me

From hole-in-the wall parties, to dating different guys, I thought I was living the great life. I loved the Lord, but He wasn't my number one priority. It was all about me and what I wanted until one day something I never expected occurred. Abortion was not an option. Adoption was not an option. Giving birth to the human growing inside me was the only option.

I was astonished from the news. I couldn't believe such a thing could happen to me. Becoming pregnant was not in my plans until after marriage, the traditional way. The day I found out I was expecting, I went to the doctor because my cycle was 4 weeks late. It was there I received the pink slip of my due date. My pregnancy was not planned at all. I went from happy, to nervous, to scared and back to happy. Those emotions played in my thoughts for a while until I went to share the news with my boyfriend and family. My boyfriend was the person I decided to share the news with first. He was a really quiet guy, so I was unsure of the type of response I was going to receive from him that day. Overall, he didn't show a lot of emotions, but he basically allowed me to decide what was best for my life.

Next, I went to my family, whom I was living with at the time, to share the unexpected news. Let's just say I didn't receive the expected answer, but I knew I had to come up with a plan B. I knew the family was embarrassed from what occurred, but I knew whatever decision I made was going to be the choice I had to live with for the rest of my life. Finally, I made the decision based on what I felt was right in my spirit. I chose to save my child only to find out later that she would be a blessing to many in the years to come.

Everything was going well with my pregnancy until my fourth month. One day, out of the blue, my boyfriend decided to let me know that he was ready to end our relationship. It was the most devastating news of my life. I cried every night, thinking, "Why were all these things happening to me?" I went through a light period of depression.

Confused, frustrated, not knowing what to do, I finally came to the conclusion that I will one day be raising this child by myself. I knew we weren't ready for marriage but I still thought there was a chance that we could make it. Even though I knew having a baby out of wedlock was wrong, I still believed that God could turn my situation around.

My first child, Kierra, was born. I prayed every night to God, not only for a healthy baby, but also a healthy relationship between her father and me. There are too many mothers and fathers fighting over custody issues, neglect from the biological parent and therefore, I did not want any part of it. Before the baby was born, we became friends again. After the baby was born we moved in with each other, but it didn't work. In the end, we never got back together but we have a great relationship for the well-being of our child, who we share together. From this experience, I came to the conclusion if we would only put God first in all things and seek Him concerning His will for our lives, He will guide us in our decisions and choices we make in life.

There are many women in the world today who are experiencing the same thing that I have experienced in my past relationship. We find ourselves in relationships that are not God- ordained but ordained by our own reasoning. Relationships can keep you bound to your enemy, or your past, if you refuse to let go. Sometimes you have to make decisions based on the outcome of things you may have dealt with from this individual. If it's not working, I learned to move on. I never thought I would become a single mother, but with God on my side, I was able to push through my pain and struggles.

After having my baby girl, it was a struggle. I knew what it felt like to be a loner. At times it was discouraging to deal with the outcome of my situation, knowing in my heart that I was not ready financially to take care of a child by myself. Often thinking that I couldn't make it, one day a peace came over me. I had to get my mind right. When you're in a state of loneliness and depression, you don't think about the goodness of Jesus. I was young and unprepared. I didn't have a plan, a thought, or a way out, but I had Jesus. Along with Jesus came wisdom, strength, and courage. I'm here to tell you, whenever you're going through, you need to read Philippians 4:13, "I can do all things through Christ which strengtheneth me." Repeat it until you feel it in your spirit. I didn't know this scripture back then, but I'm here to say that this scripture has helped me keep my sanity. This scripture has given me hope until now. I didn't have a cheerleading team saying, "You can do it!" It was God's grace that kept me. Don't ever feel like you are alone. God is here with you to help you carry the burden. He tells us to cast our cares upon Him. As women, we need to learn not to carry so much weight. Never tell yourself you are a failure. Never tell yourself you can't do it.

After my boyfriend and I broke up, I kept the apartment for the remainder of the year. In 2003, I moved to a based-on-income apartment community because I was financially unable to handle the load by myself. Moving alone and depending on one income to take care of two people was a struggle. Standing in the food stamp line and getting assistance was the most embarrassing thing I thought I could have done. I'm not knocking the help, before I got pregnant, I never saw myself getting help from the government. I tried really hard to stay afloat, but it seems like the harder I tried the more I drowned.

I was a hardworking, single mother who always kept a decent paying job. I often worked two jobs to make ends meet and still didn't have enough, but God made away. The guys I dated were no help at all. They couldn't help with out with any bills. I guess at the end of the day, they didn't live with me so why should I expect them to help me? Struggling to keep up with my bills, I could have turned to other measures to make extra money by prostituting or working for a strip club, but I didn't. I could have easily taken that path, but all I could think about was my daughter. I did not want my child to grow up and hear about the ungodly actions

I took in life to keep a roof over our heads. There is a saying, "you got to do what you got to do to make it happen", but I also do believe in morals and principles. I had to set a standard for myself. My reputation has always been important to me.

There were people who could have helped. I had some wealthy and stable friends, mostly male; however, if you weren't giving anything in return, then they couldn't help your need and I don't call people like that friends. I would often ask if I could borrow the money, but they insisted, "Why borrow when you can have it all?" The offer sounded good, but I would have been considered a prostitute. Many may not agree, but if you're sleeping with a male, receiving money from him, and there is no dating involved, you are prostituting yourself.

During those years of struggling, I grew weak. I wanted to give up. The weight was too overbearing for me at times. The system said I was making too much money so I was eventually taken off assistance because my two jobs increased my salary beyond the allotted limit.

After two years of living this path, I called on the Lord and He heard my cry. In my spirit I felt a need to change. I begin to pray and cry out to the Lord, "Lord, why am I going through all of this?" After months of praying, I felt the presence of the Lord with me. I was able to hear Him. God began to deal with me about some things. He showed me the reason I was struggling. The devil was trying to make a bid for my life, but God had a plan for me. Satan knew that if He could have claimed victory over my soul then he would have used me for his glory.

I just had to make a change. The area where I lived was horrible. I was living in an area that was filled with lust, drugs, sex, and heavy demonic activity. These forces were trying to overpower me. When I moved into the neighborhood, I told myself that I would not end up like the rest. I pleaded with God to change my living conditions. I knew I didn't belong in a place like that. I believe God allowed me to go to such a place so I could see how my life would end if I didn't get myself together. I don't think that I would have ended up on drugs, but I probably wouldn't have succeeded in life. I am not putting anyone down for living on government assistance, but if you don't see yourself living beyond your "free" apartment, food system, and state-supported checks, then your mind and your life can be relegated to a small box. You may think that you don't deserve better, but you do.

Romans 12:1–2 says, *"I appeal to you therefore, brothers, by the mercies of God, to present your bodies as a living sacrifice, holy and acceptable to God, which is your reasonable service. Do not be conformed to this world, but be transformed by the renewal of your mind, that by testing you may discern what is the will of God, what is good and acceptable and perfect."*

If you aren't careful, the enemy will try to cover your big vision with a small vision. Know that you deserve better. That's why it is so important for you to renew your mind on a daily basis. The Bible tells us to die daily to this flesh (1 Cor, 15:31). You have to think positively about yourself to know that you deserve better. Even though I was driving to a hole-in-the-wall place, I pulled into the parking lot everyday like it was going to be my last day. I can remember pulling up and people staring at me because they knew I didn't belong. I had two vehicles, wore designer clothing from head to toe and never looked like I was lacking for anything. I worked hard to get back on my feet. You can live in the hood but you don't have to become the hood. You don't have to become that person that is selling drugs, gang-banging or selling their bodies. You have a chance to do better.

I'm a living witness that whenever you get to your lowest, like Job in the Bible, and it seems as if everything has been stripped from you, you can overcome. Just look at your situation as a temporary thing and not a long-term situation. It's all up to you. If you change your thoughts, you can change your situation. I had to believe in myself. What you believe about yourself is what you will become. You have to know that you are special. Things will happen in your life but it will not be your ending outcome. You need to desire to change. God will move based on what's in your heart. Your outer appearance will deceive many but God is looking at what's on the inside. He knows who is ready for a change and He will bless you accordingly.

God began to prepare my new life, the life He had already predestined for me. I slowed down on the dating and remained single. Finally in 2004, I met the man I would one day marry. My future husband was on a job interview at the school where I was employed at that time. When he walked in to view the classroom, something told me to look up. So I looked up and saw a slim, tall, dark-skinned male at the doorway of the classroom. "Okay" and "what", were the two words that came to me. I caught myself staring at him and so did a co-worker. I remember her saying, "Jennifer, what are you looking at? You know that he is not your type." My response was, "I know, right?" So the gentleman walked by us, but I noticed there was something different about this guy that I couldn't put my finger on.

The young gentleman got hired at the school and became one of the youngest black male assistant principals in the school district. Years went by and I was still alone. Often I desired to get back into the dating game, not knowing God had the perfect one right before my eyes. I only saw him as a coworker at the school, and we often just spoke to each other while passing in the halls. What was really funny was that I knew other women on the job were checking him out!

One day, he came to me and asked for some assistance with an outside project. I was well-known for helping others put excellent projects together, so he asked for my assistance on a particular task. I didn't know he was a pastor until he explained the project to me. He needed some assistance with his church advertisement. I thought, "What in the world…?" I said, "Lord, You got be kidding me." At that time, I didn't realize what God was doing. I thought to myself, "With all the wicked and sinful things I have done, I don't want to touch such an anointed task." Finally I built my courage and completed the project.

He was very pleased with my work and invited me to a church service. At first I was a bit hesitant, but I went and then continued to visit off and on. Still, I didn't have any special feeling about this guy. We began to chat here and there, only offering encouragement to one another. He was going through some things and so was I. We became closer at that point. God began to do great things in both of our lives. He was later promoted to be principal of another school.

We eventually married and things began to fall in place for us. I thank God for allowing me to see that I deserved better in life. My husband was waiting for me. God has a mate for you as well. It took me giving up the fleshly desires and wanting the things of God. It wasn't about the material things in life. God was trying to get my attention the whole time. I finally saw the warning signs that I was heading for destruction. I thank God for the path I took. It wasn't a straight path but in the crooked places is where I learned who I am. My struggles made me stronger and wiser. I am a better woman for my husband and children. Our marriage has not always been the best, but we pressed through the many obstacles we faced to make it.

I praise God for my husband because he also helped me in so many ways. When I was down, he spoke words of encouragement. When I was depressed, he spoke life. He was there for me when family couldn't understand. My life was in a complete wreck, but the Lord saw fit to restore me. My husband could have left me, but instead he constantly prayed and fasted for my healing. The devil tried to destroy me, but God had a plan. He still tried to take me down, but God saw fit for me to live. There was too much value in me to throw away. God placed a ministry inside of me that would one day be a blessing to others. Now that I am healed, God has used me in ways I would have never known.

This road hasn't been easy but at the end of my journey I want to hear the Lord say, "Well done, my daughter." I want to encourage you today, that if this testimony sounds like your story, you can ask God right now to set you free. Your life doesn't have to end the way it began. Just like the Lord has a plan for you, the devil has one too. His plan is to destroy you. He doesn't want to see you live. He wants your soul. He wants your mind. He wants your thoughts. You do have a choice in life. You can live right and go to heaven or you can live in sin and go to hell. I have never been to hell in the spirit, but when I allowed the devil to use me, I felt the heat of hell. I was to the point of surrendering my soul until I saw the light.

Just because you may be at the bottom right now, don't ever feel like you can't float to the top. You have a choice. I pray that you choose to live. God needs you. He's waiting for a "Yes". I can remember telling the Lord, "Yes, I surrender to your will." God was calling me into His Kingdom. I felt within that I had to give it all up. Because I was willing to go to a place in God that others didn't desire, I had to change the way I was living. If God was going to use me to break generational curses, I had to be free myself. I had to go through a deliverance process in order to be a help to others.

The Bible tells us that some things come out by fasting and prayer (Matthew 17:21). It took fasting, praying, laying of the hands, self-recognition and, God to break through some barriers and strongholds that had taken root in my life. Sometimes we have to admit that we have addictions or problems that are too big to solve on our own. Many of you can say you can handle it all by yourselves, but when those demonic spirits have multiplied, the fight is greater.

You will play a significant part in your own deliverance. You will need to be able to identify the strongholds and denounce them. In doing so, you will definitely have to maintain a clear mind because you will have spirits mentally fighting you, telling you that you're okay. Ask God to reveal what is keeping you bound from moving forward. If you're too frightened to know, then seek help from a godly believer or your pastor.

When you are living a sinful lifestyle, the root cause of your behavior could be based on a spirit(s) that is in your family. People in your family, or bloodline, could have done some wicked things. But if God is able to save you out of your whole family, with fasting and prayer, you will then be able to pray for deliverance for the rest of your family members. God wants you to be an example for the rest. Many may desire to be free from sin but don't know how. God will allow His spirit to operate in you to reach out to them. As long as we live a wicked, sinful lifestyle, we are allowing the devil to take control over our lives. He is literally draining the life out of God's people.

In our church, we constantly deal with the subject of spiritual warfare because many don't realize that they are fighting battles on the inside. The battle could be from bad childhood memories, sexual abuse, un-forgiveness, or from any type of trauma they may have experienced along the way. We have to tackle these issues. Stop covering up the pain with a Band-Aid, and ask God for healing. What I notice in the Body of Christ is that the people who have experienced suffering, pain or trauma, are more likely to cause trouble in the church if they don't allow God to heal them of their wounds. They often call themselves the victims when actually, they may be the one initiating the problem. As a church, we need to deal with these issues. Often, people may know they need help but refuse to reach out for assistance.

If we continue to live with issues and not reach out for help, we could end up living in a cycle of bitterness, hatred and resentment. These issues can bring sickness upon you. God tells us to cast our cares upon Him. Don't allow past hurts keep you from moving forward. I know it's hard to move on after we have been hurt, but allowing the pain to grow with your spirit will grieve the Holy Spirit.

Sometimes we just have to let it go even though we want to find an answer to the problem. You may never understand why you were affected, but you need to release the pain to God. If you think you are in bondage, ask God what is holding you.

Take a moment to reflect on your childhood. Here are some questions that you can ask yourself to help you discover the stronghold that may be keeping you from being free:

Did you feel left out or mistreated as a child?

Did your parent(s) treat you equally with your other siblings?

Were you bullied?

Were you sexually abused?

Did you fail a grade level in school?

Did you complete college?

Was your spouse caught in adultery?

Did your spouse leave or divorced you?

Have you completed any of your goals?

Are you withholding forgiveness from someone who has hurt or offended you?

These are questions that can open the door to the negative thoughts you may perceive in your mind. If you have answered, "yes" to any of the questions, I do advise you to seek the Lord concerning these issues. You may be walking around with a character trait that was formed due to some type of mistreatment, abuse, or pain. Many have walked around with pain so long, it has become a part of them. In church we often see that people will attend with a different attitude each Sunday. You will never know how they will react or respond given the situation. If this describes you, I am telling you to seek help today. Allow God to speak to you concerning your deliverance. Focus on the areas in your life that were damaged from an event in your past. If you don't seek the Lord concerning this matter, you can damage yourself, others and your children if you have wounds that remain unhealed.

It is my desire to see my family, your family, and people around the world set free. I pray every day that God will break the yoke of the enemy off the life of my family. Many are blind to the fact that the devil is using them to cause harm to themselves and others. I'm set free because I desired to be free. You have that same choice. Choose to live. Choose to be an instrument for the Kingdom. God may not be calling you into the pulpit, but He's calling you to be a believer in Him. You can do all things because WHEN YOU BELIEVE IN God, you will receive supernatural power to do whatever you put your mind to. I didn't have anything going on in my life until I truly met our Lord and Savior Jesus Christ.

This is not the story of the perfect wife; it's a story with a perfect ending.

CHAPTER TWO
Questions for Consideration

How important is your relationship with Christ?

Does the Lord have your undivided attention?

Are you living for Christ or the world?

What is hindering you from going forward?

Do you believe you have the power to overcome the things that you are trying to leave behind?

Scriptures of Reflection

1 Corinthians 10:13 There hath no temptation taken you but such as is common to man: but God [is] faithful, who will not suffer you to be tempted above that ye are able; but will with the temptation also make a way to escape, that ye may be able to bear [it].

1 John 1:9 If we confess our sins, he is faithful and just to forgive us [our] sins, and to cleanse us from all unrighteousness.

Romans 3:23 For all have sinned, and come short of the glory of God...

James 5:16 Confess [your] faults one to another, and pray one for another, that ye may be healed. The effectual fervent prayer of a righteous man availeth much.

James 2:8 If ye fulfill the royal law according to the scripture, Thou shalt love thy neighbor as thyself, ye do well...

Acts 22:16 And now why tarriest thou? Arise, and be baptized, and wash away thy sins, calling on the name of the Lord.

CHAPTER THREE

Walking in Deliverance

Since this book is about my life, I want to take a moment to share with you some things that have kept me from being free of my past. I never knew the decisions I made earlier in life would have such an impact on my life today.

We all make mistakes in our lives. Some choices we make are based on our decisions and other choices we make are brought about through circumstances, relationships, friends and family.

Yes, we have the right to make our own decisions, but do we ever stop to think that these decisions would one day affect our lives and people around us? Different news sites and social media are always announcing a negative report on someone. As people, in our human nature, we are always looking for some type of news, the latest gossip, or the recent drama. Someone is always looking to expose you by bringing up the old "you". It could be things you have done, tried, or thought about. It can be something from 20 years ago; it will somehow make its way to the surface somewhere in your lifetime. The conversation always starts with "remember you used to…?" I learned not to get into that type of conversation because some things you just want to forget and move on. I look at it this way, if it can be used as a testimony then I will share it, but if you're going to take my testimony as something to gossip about then my lips are sealed. I'm often private about certain things as it pertains to my life because I learned everybody can't handle your testimony.

    Many people walk around today believing that God can't use a sinner, drug dealer, thief, etc. Before we judge, we need to think about our own short-comings. Life is different now than from fifty years ago. The crime rate has increased, young girls are having babies earlier, and diseases are spreading more rapidly. Things are changing in the world. We can sit around and talk about the statistics, but as a person, what can you do to help bring about a change? I can't change what someone has done in their past, but as an individual, I always consult God on how I can help them pick up the pieces and move on.

As adults, we don't realize the choices we make in life can affect our family, friends, community, and the nation. For instance, if a mother is on drugs while pregnant, there is a possibility that the child may have some type of disability. When people make decisions to drop out of school, it can have an effect on their career. The separation of parents can take a toll on a child's education, and even future, for their own families.

Think about the choices that you make on a day to day basis, because the decisions are not only about you but also others.

After I graduated from high school, I made the wrong choice to have sex without first being married and it resulted in some loss. I felt like I lost everything I had gained. I had a long list of goals that I had wanted to accomplish by the time I turned forty. I mean, I had it all planned out like most of you. My dreams were as large as I could imagine them. Because of my choices in life, what I had on paper didn't match up with the completed outcome. Even though I made wrong choices in life, I asked God to forgive me and praised Him for the seed that I was able to birth forth. My children may not have the same father in the natural, but they do have the same Father in heaven, and at the end of the day, that is all that matters.

Think about these questions below. There are so many things that can affect our lives and others around us.

Think about these questions:
-If I drink alcohol, how can it affect me in the long run?
-If I smoke cigarettes, what would happen to my lungs years from now?
-If I do drugs, what type of effect will they have on my body or mind?
-If I commit murder, who will be affected?
-If I commit adultery, who will I hurt?
-If I have unprotected sex, without being married, what could take place?
-If I become a member of a gang (occults, etc.) what could happen to me?
-If I do anything that is contrary to the word of God what would or could happen?

These are the things that we should think about when we make decisions. They may seem like the pleasures of life but we should always question, "Why am I doing this?" Think about the outcome and not just the moment.

There may be some things that you are struggling with right now. If you have a desire to stop doing something that is not in the will of God, then that is the Holy Spirit nudging you to stop.

After graduating from high school, my life did a 180° turn. I had dreams, I had plans and I had goals. Making the wrong decisions caused a down fall in my life and opened a door for the enemy. I don't know if you are aware of the pit. It's a place where you wouldn't want your soul to be trapped. The devil will design a trap that you may think is impossible to escape.

I can remember the day I told the Lord that I'm leaving this life behind. It was the year 2003 when I met a young man at the dollar store. We exchanged numbers and went about our business. I didn't have any interest in this guy, but I took the number for conversation and maybe dinner. We talked on the phone, maybe two or three times, and he seemed like a nice guy. I didn't see any red flags so when he called one particular evening and said he was in the area, I told him he could bring me some donuts. Well, I got the donuts and a whole lot of other things! Before he came to my home, I had a strange feeling.

Like the old folks used to say, "Something in the milk ain't clean". So before he came in, I somewhat had a feeling about a gun. Not knowing his past, I asked him, out of the blue, was he "packing"? Packing means to carry a weapon. I didn't ask to see the gun because I was too terrified, but when he confirmed he did have a gun, I remained calm. I was a little scared, but at the same time, I knew I had to come up with a plan quickly. Thoughts began to rush through my mind. I thought about my daughter, family, life and dreams.

I immediately told the Lord, "If you help me get him out of my house, I promise I will stop doing all the wrong things and live totally for You." So, I was prompted on what to do next. While remaining calm, not showing him any fear, I politely told him I was tired and was preparing to call it a night. He was over for less than fifteen minutes, but those minutes seemed the longest ever. He couldn't understand, but he agreed to leave. "Thank the Lord", I thought to myself. He said, "I'm leaving, but you promise this is not the last time I will see you again?" Deep down inside I knew it was the final time, but I told him, "Sure, I will call you later." So before he left, he wanted me to make a promise. I told him we don't need to make a promise, he will hear from me. But he was persistent. He wanted to make a blood promise. When he stated, "blood promise", I immediately knew something wasn't right and not to do it. So I then asked if he was in a gang and he stated he was affiliated with a gang and that's why he was always carrying a weapon. I told him I don't deal with that type of group.

The fear in me was about to show, so I then told him I'm not going to shake hands on the promise, but I will keep in contact with him. He finally stopped asking for a promise and then asked for hug. As he was coming towards me, the shape of his face and eyes had changed. He started to look like a snake and tried to kiss me and at the time I pushed him away and told him I would rather not. Thank God he didn't try anymore and left on peaceful terms. I never saw the young man again, but I knew that day I was playing with darkness and surrendered my all unto the Lord. When I sit back and think about the times I was being gullible, it could have cost me my life.

Take the time to think about something you want to get out of. If you put your mind to it you can break through any barrier. You will need to have your mind made up and your heart in the right place. Then allow the Holy Spirit to separate your spirit from the desires of the flesh. Galatians 2:20 says, "I am crucified with Christ: nevertheless I live; yet not I, but Christ liveth in me: and the life which I now live in the flesh I live by the faith of the Son of God, who loved me, and gave himself for me". It is time to live free! You shall be an overcomer! You shall live and not die! You shall speak things that are not as though they were! You shall use the power God has given you to stomp on the devil's head! You shall have life and have life more abundantly! God has made you the head and not the tail!

I speak strength and faith into your life right now in the name of Jesus! You shall live free from all sin in Jesus name!

CHAPTER THREE
Questions for Consideration

Reflect back to your past. If you could change one situation from your past what would it be?

How do you plan to live your life in a more positive way?

Take some time to think about the choices you are currently making. Now, think how they will affect others around you.

What is your most memorable testimony?

Scriptures of Reflection

Exodus 20:5 Thou shalt not bow down thyself to them, nor serve them: for I the LORD thy God [am] a jealous God, visiting the iniquity of the fathers upon the children unto the third and fourth [generation] of them that hate me;

James 5:16 Confess [your] faults one to another, and pray one for another, that ye may be healed. The effectual fervent prayer of a righteous man availeth much.

Numbers 14:18 The LORD [is] longsuffering, and of great mercy, forgiving iniquity and transgression, and by no means clearing [the guilty], visiting the iniquity of the fathers upon the children unto the third and fourth [generation].

CHAPTER FOUR

He Chose Me

The life of an Elect Lady is unexplainable. Many people ask, "How can you do all the things that you do?" We wear many hats, being the pastor's wife. We hold several positions or help out in many parts of the ministry. Not to take over, but to assist the ministers to help things run more smoothly for our spouses. This role does not come with a book of directions, but I allowed God to prepare me as He saw fit. I was young going into the marriage, but the Lord said He would be by my side every step of the way. I eventually grew into the role of Elect Lady.

God changed everything about me: the way I talked, the way I dressed, the way I carried myself, my surroundings and my friends. The old me was washed away. Because of where God brought me from, people laughed and seemed surprised when they heard I was marrying a preacher. They doubted that my marriage would even last a year. I do know this: God can take nothing and make something out of it. Just like Adam was created with the dust of the earth, God re-created me. People have to remember that God is the Creator. He can create, reshape, and make things no man can.

    I actually count it a blessing to not only be married, but married to an awesome man of God. We are able to be there for one another. I'm his helpmate along with the Helper, the Holy Spirit. It's an honor to serve my husband. When he's down, I'm there to help lift him up. If I'm having a problem or a bad day, he's right there to encourage me. Yes, I do get tired and weary at times, but I know that the Lord won't put more on me than I can bear.

> *Proverbs 18:22 {Whoso} findeth a wife findeth a good {thing}, and obtaineth favour of the Lord.*

    On July 23, 2006, I became the Elect Lady of Global Outreach Ministries-Healing & Deliverance Ministry, formerly known as Clark Ministries.

    I was excited to be married. Unaware of the spiritual part of being married, I wasn't thrilled about the warfare that came along with the call. I didn't know if I could fit the shoes I would one day be walking in. As the wife of a pastor, I dealt with some serious issues and have seen the unexpected happen.

Walter and I got married fairly quickly. The devil didn't want our marriage to happen at all. We had all kinds of battles. People didn't want our marriage to work, but the Bible says, "What therefore God hath joined together, let not man put asunder" (Mark 10:9). In spite of everyone's opinions, we tied the knot without a formal wedding. I always desired to have a large wedding, but from the looks of it, there would have been no wedding or just a small wedding. All I knew is that I was not going to let anyone or anything stop us from being together. Before people could think about it or talk about it, it was a done deal. Finally, in the year 2011, we renewed our vows and had an official wedding. Everyone was invited to the ceremony. Even the ones who thought we weren't going to make it attended and were welcomed to be a part of our special day. It was the best day ever!

I knew being married to a pastor wasn't going to be the easiest thing to do. Before I got married, I was going through a healing process from issues I had undergone in my past, and on top of that, I had to transition into walking in an unexpected calling. Many people have judged me, and even thought I was unworthy of the calling, but we all have fallen short somewhere. 1John 1:9 "If we confess our sins, he is faithful and just to forgive us our sins, and to cleanse us from all unrighteousness." I know plenty of people who have done wrong, but I am here to say that if you ask God to forgive you, He will. There is still time. No one on earth is perfect, but as Christians, we tend to forget that we were once fornicators, liars, backsliders, thieves, gamblers, devil-worshippers, gold-diggers, club hoppers, moonshine drinkers, accusers, and the list goes on.

I have seen and learnt so much as an Elect Lady, the pastor's wife. The warfare has been intense, but I can't throw in my towel now. I remember a time when Walter and I were just acquaintances. During this time, a particular visitor was interested in him. He met this woman because he offered prayer to one of her relatives. So, Walter invites her to service, as usual. The lady came out to several services as a result. Every time she came, I noticed something strange about her. She was much older than I, but I often wondered why she had an issue with me? It's like our spirits were fighting against each other. The woman started doing her hair like mine, and dressing in similar clothes, trying to look like me. Was I freaking out? Oh yes! That was the beginning of my journey before becoming Elect Lady Clark.

Was I prepared for this role? No. I don't think you can ever be prepared to be an Elect Lady. You can read manuals on how to be a wife, but there's no manual on how to be an Elect Lady. Am I the best Elect Lady? Many people would probably have different opinions. Am I doing the best I can to support my husband and the ministry? I would be glad to answer that question with a "Yes!" There is a price to pay to walk in the shoes of any woman; however, the Elect Lady gets it all.

I have been judged, criticized, mistreated, talked about, lied on and all the above. I am still standing tall because of the grace of God. God has given me sufficient grace to deal with many opposing forces and the battles that come along with this position.

There are times that I just wanted to say, "I quit, I can't take it anymore". I often sit and cry due to the amount of pressure that I am constantly under. I can't speak for all pastor's wives but we go through things that others can't imagine. I am constantly dealing with issues from other women. Whether its jealousy, disrespect, immaturity, being who others want me to be or dealing with women desiring to be with my husband. These are the behind-the-scenes issues that many women face being the pastor's wife, but I want to write this book to let other women know that they're not alone.

I can remember a time when the devil used a person to attack me. She did all she could do to ruin my character with lie after lie and plot after plot, but the Lord revealed the plan to me. The plan was to destroy me. The battle went on for a long time - almost a year. The devil wanted me out of the picture. I don't know if anyone has ever been through something like this before, but it is not a good feeling to feel like you're helpless. If someone is talking about you or saying untrue things, you want to defend yourself. I couldn't do anything in this situation. It was beyond my human control.

All along I knew this was going on, but I felt like I was trapped. I didn't have anyone to confide in because people would have thought I was crazy. Finally, I said "Lord I can't do this anymore," but the Lord said, "Yes you can, now hang in there." It was hard to sit back and allow people to ruin your name or to come against you. I never thought I would experience such things, but they happened. Don't let this scare you because these types of things happen on a daily basis to all people. Titles don't have anything to do with the devil's assignments. He doesn't care anything about you. He just wants your soul, your thoughts, and your body.

I often just wanted to walk away from it all. I wasn't thinking suicide, but I was thinking about divorce. I wondered if it would be easier for me to pack up and disappear. I was not afraid of being alone. Remember, I was an independent woman so going back to being single would have been easier for me. No drama, just me and my kids. What would I have accomplished by running from the enemy? These types of situations happen in the church and out of the church.

At the end of the day, I knew the spirit that was working behind the individual. I knew the plot of the enemy. The plan was to destroy everything that I had worked hard for, including my family and the ministry, and to kill me spiritually. Ladies, if you dealt with a situation like this, or a similar one, I am here to let you know that the Lord is with you. You will have a season where things would be smooth sailing and then you will have a down season, feeling that it can't get better. There will be times when you will have to fight spiritually and at other times pray and listen to the Lord.

That year was the toughest of them all, but I made it, not knowing I was in the pruning season of my ministry! The devil had a plan, but God had a test and I passed it. I didn't give in. I stayed the course. That is what we have to do. Stand firm in the tornadoes; stand tall in the battle; and stand still when needed.

Some things in life will be a test and others will come in your life to knock you off course. I was hurt, but I'm allowing God to heal the wounds. Many of us are walking around with unhealed wounds due to relationships, marriages, abuse, and neglect. I'm not writing this only for pastor's wives, but for all women. The enemy is out trying to deceive, kill, and destroy, but the Lord said that He has come so that we can have life.

To all women, keep your husband in prayer. Whether he is a preacher, doctor, lawyer, janitor, cable man... cover your loved one in prayer. Travail for your mate. Don't allow the devil to destroy what God has given you.

As I write, I'm reminded of Job. The devil took everything Job owned, but he couldn't take Job's faith. He took away his animals, crops, wealth and loved ones; but in the end, Job came out on top. Put your faith in God and it will be alright. Surround yourself with positive, praying people; the people that God has called in your life for a purpose. When you're down, they can, with the help of the Lord, uplift, encourage, and speak life into you. There are some people who say things just because it sounds right. There are others who really see that you're going through hardship, but when you feel genuine love, you know that it is God. You don't have to be a prophet, prophetess, apostle, or any other type of leader to see the needs of others. If you have the Holy Spirit on the inside, you often feel the person's spirit.

In spite of my trials, I still give God the praise. I felt like giving in, giving up, and walking out, but He kept me. For the things I didn't know, He gave me wisdom. There are areas where I once was weak, but God made me strong. When my eyes were closed to things, He allowed me to see. He is shaping and molding me into a beautiful piece of His creation. I am still on the potter's wheel being molded into the woman He desires me to be.

We are to set an example for women in our churches, communities and in our homes. I knew a day would come when my old ways would pass away and the new woman, on the inside of me, would rise to the surface. I gave up a lot of things to walk in my calling. I can remember my last visit to the club. I was hanging out with my friends on a cold, winter night. We didn't care how cold or hot it was outside, we just got our partying on! Dancing with my high heel boots, I didn't realize that it would be my last time on the dance floor. I'm off the dance floor and now I'm dancing for the Lord. It's shouting time now, no more "turning up" in the club, it's all about coming to the house of God to worship our Heavenly Father.

This is the season where the Lord is pulling His women to the front line. If you were overlooked by many, God is saying to you on this day, "Daughter, I am calling you forth." God is calling you to a higher place. He is calling you to a new level in Him. Begin to step out on faith. He will not let you fall. If it seems like you're falling, He's got you.

It was faith that kept me. Not knowing how I was going to do it all, faith allowed me to depend totally upon God. Even when I ran out of energy to keep up, it was my faith that kept pushing me. With a demanding schedule, my husband and I managed to keep things together. Often spending time away from each other, we definitely made sure we communicated with one another. Without communication, our bond would have never grown stronger. It is important to put family first no matter how busy our lives may become.

I lost a lot of friends after I got married. Some were for good reasons and others due to the time I was unable to spend on the phone or visiting with them. Seven days a week, we were always doing something. My close relatives also began to think I was losing my mind. I didn't visit, call, or write; I was just in my own little world, doing the work of the Lord. My mind was so focused on being the perfect wife that I neglected my own needs. Putting all the focus on my husband, children and ministry, my personal life was not important anymore. I was spending less time in prayer. I began to worry more because I wanted everything right to please my husband, making sure he and the children had everything they needed. When you are married to a minister, your needs often get pushed to the side. It can be a hard task, trying to balance family matters, raising children, working, going to school, and keeping up with home. The list could go on and on.

Feeling overwhelmed, I wanted to say, "I quit." This was too much for one person. If you are married, think about the work you do as wife plus assisting with ministry. With all these things to do, I felt my relationship with the Lord wasn't as strong as I desired it to be. I then realized what was going on. I put everything else before God. Yes, God wants me to serve my husband, but my relationship with the Lord should be my number one priority. If I would have prayed to the Lord about these problems instead of trying to handle them on my own, then I wouldn't have felt so besieged. Realizing I couldn't do it on my own, the Lord began to show me how to prioritize my day. My day began with Him and the rest just flowed.

The Lord not only helped me with strategizing my day, He also provided for needs in the ministry. He began to send people to the ministry and they later became members. These members came in and began to help right away. Hallelujah, the load had finally been lifted! Being the pastor's wife is a calling which can often be overlooked by others. People don't understand the work that goes on behind the scenes. Not only are you required to assist your spouse, but you also face challenges from the congregation. Ministry is a calling and also a job. As an Elect Lady, even if you feel that you are not called into the ministry to preach, the members are still looking to you for help. I have also gone through a lot dealing with hurt people in the church. Every person who walks through the doors of the church needs some type of help. There are many Christians walking around with unhealed wounds, not knowing they are affecting others. People who have been abused (physically, emotionally, and mentality), can hurt themselves and others. It is important to expose your wounds. You can have a spiritual disease that can hurt others and yourself. Ask God to begin the healing in your mind, body and soul.

CHAPTER FOUR
Questions for Consideration

Are you disqualifying yourself from God's purposes because of your past mistakes?

Are things recurring in your life? Are you wondering why you keep going through the same thing?

Are you always blaming others for your problems? Can you be the problem? Why or Why not?

Are you open to feedback from God?

If you have been hurt and desire healing, what can you do to begin the healing process? How can you stay free from the hurt that was once a part of your life?

Scriptures of Reflection

In order to be that woman God has called you to be, He has given us some guidelines to live by:

We should live a holy lifestyle (2 Peter 1:3)

Be a follower of Christ (Ephesians 5:1)

Be a Godly woman/wife (Proverbs 31:10)

Keep our spirits pure and clean (Romans 12:1, 2)

Be able to love (John 7:24)

Have integrity (James 4:10)

Be a positive person (Psalms 71:8)

Be a prayer warrior (Proverbs 31)

Be a team player (Romans 13:13)

Be an intercessor/worshipper (John 4:24)

Learn to cover your spouse (Proverbs 31:11, 12)

Be an aide in the ministry ((Proverbs 31:26)

Be a role model (Proverbs 31:13-22)

Be a friend to all (Matthew 5:42-45)

Prayer

Lord, I pray that my spouse will make you the Lord of his life. Let him have the mind of Christ and be led by the Holy Spirit and not his flesh. Keep his eyes away from temptations that he will not sin. Allow him to hear your still voice. Let everything he speaks be pleasing to you.

I pray he will humble himself before You that he may be strong, courageous, and vigilant to do everything that is written in Your Word, so that he will live a thriving and triumphant life. Keep him healthy that he will enjoy the work of his hands and see it as a gift from You.

Lord, let him stand firm in his faith and not waver. Help him stay true to our marriage vows and that our love will never fade. Amen.

CHAPTER FIVE

Pregnant with Possibilities

And the angel of the LORD appeared unto the woman, and said unto her, Behold now, thou art barren, and bearest not: but thou shalt conceive, and bear a son. Judges 13:3 KJV

Like Manoah's wife, God spoke to me and said, "You shall birth many daughters and women, in the spirit, and around the world." Because I have laid down my own life to submit to His will, He is using my life to bring deliverance, healing, and hope to women of all nationalities. It is no longer what Jennifer wants to do but what God wants me to do. It can be the same way for you. You have to choose and allow God to have His way in your life.

We, as women, need to understand that God has a purpose and plan for our lives. When I was clubbing and partying back in the days, God still had a plan for me. When I was cursing and being disobedient, God still had a plan for me. You may be going through difficulties right now, but God has already predetermined your life before you were even born. Opening up a child care center has always been one of my dreams. Working with children was one of my callings in life. I have had the opportunity to work with so many children. I first started working with children while I was in high school and went to college to further my career in the field of Early Childhood Education. With over 13 years of experience teaching children of all ages, somewhere along the way, I felt that I too, one day, would be able to run my own school.

My last job really motivated me to pursue my dream. I was having so many issues on my job at that particular time, I said, "Lord, it has to get better than this." Many prophets spoke this day care into existence, but my faith was not up to par. God sometimes will put you into a place or allow circumstances to drive you out of your comfort zone. I knew I couldn't bare it any longer so I started planning behind the scenes. When God gives you the "okay", you better believe He's going to back you up. In the year of 2009, the Lord spoke to me and said, "Daughter whatever you ask in my name, it shall be given." Even though I had permission from the Lord to go forward with the plan, I was a little timid, but I was encouraged by my husband and friends to step out on faith. So I prayed about it and prayed some more. Finally, I turned in my resignation letter. In January of 2010, I resigned from being a teacher and transitioned into being a business owner. It is 2014 and my doors are still open for business. We serve a mighty God. The number of children has been up and down but my family has never missed a meal. The Bible says in 1 Peter 5:7 "Casting all your care upon him; for he careth for you." Every time I get down or get discouraged, I remember to put all my problems and worries into God's hand.

We don't know much about Manoah's wife. She wasn't the most popular lady but God chose her to give birth to one of the greatest judges during those days. We may seem unpopular to others, even unworthy at times, but in God's eyes we are precious. People may not know your name now, but one day, all shall see your face and know your name. All we know about Manoah's wife is that she was barren and married to him. An angel of the Lord came to visit her and told her that she would bear a son and soon she had Samson (Judges 13:3). As I stated earlier, we don't know her name, how she looked or much about her background, but what we do know is that God chose this unknown, barren woman to become an extraordinary mother.

She gave birth to one of the greatest warriors in biblical times. I am a living testimony that God can come into your life and turn your entire situation around. You may think that you are nothing and many may doubt who you are, but God doesn't make mistakes. If you are living in this world today, you are called with a purpose.

I was once told that I wasn't going to be anybody. We're often called ungodly names but I never let the seed of the enemy take root in my spirit. I fought every day to be somebody successful. When the enemy said I was a nobody, in 2003 God sent a prophet into my life to root out what the devil had spoken over me, canceling the enemy's plan for my life. It is now 2014, and the devil is still on my trail because I refuse to live the unholy, sinful and wicked lifestyle he (the devil) desires for me to live. The battle is tough, but I have the victory through Jesus Christ. I Corinthians 15:57 says, "But thanks be to God, which giveth us the victory through our Lord Jesus Christ."

Growing up, I struggled in many areas of my life. My family was rooted in so much sin that it was almost impossible to escape. I escaped the spirit of alcoholism, nicotine, homosexuality, fornication, adultery and many other sinful acts and deeds. Romans 12: 1-2 says, "1I beseech you therefore, brethren, by the mercies of God, that ye present your bodies a living sacrifice, holy, acceptable unto

God, which is your reasonable service. 2And be not conformed to this world: but be ye transformed by the renewing of your mind, that ye may prove what is that good, and acceptable, and perfect, will of God (KJV)." I had to separate myself. I saw the outcome of some of my family members and I just knew that wasn't where I wanted to be.

In order for me to find out who I was in Christ, I had to give up my former lifestyle. Yeah, it was fun at times and often life threatening too, but God had His angels surrounding me while I was out in the world. I was never on drugs but I hung around drug dealers and even dated a few. If God's hands weren't on my life, I would have ended up on drugs, been an alcoholic and probably a prostitute. I am not ashamed of things I've done and I'm not proud of the things I went through. I just know that there is another young lady who is walking in the shoes I once walked in and she is ready to step out. Today, if this is you, I'm here to tell you that God's hand is open and He's ready to receive you.

I was in the world, but now I can say that I have been totally delivered from the sins that once had me bound. I'm not saying that they will never taunt you, they will always tempt you, but God has given us the power to overcome the enemy and we are now able to walk in victory. You may be spiritually pregnant with a ministry, a salon, store, restaurant or children, but God does not want you to abort your destiny. No matter what you are faced with in life, God doesn't want you to abort your baby. He wants you to hold on to your dreams. God has given us all a road map for our lives and He wants you to get back on our journey so we can fulfill the purpose for our lives.

You may look at your life as if you're barren spiritually. There are many people living today who don't believe that God can do the miraculous in our lives. Whatever you do, don't believe the lie of the enemy. You were destined for greatness. Speak life into the dry areas of your life. You are not barren. There is something so great that is ready to come forth from your belly, but you have allowed the gift to lie dormant because you don't believe. When we look into God's word we find many women who were once barren:

Abraham and Sarah had given up hope of ever having their own children when God gave Abraham the promise that he and Sarah would have a son whose offspring would be greater than the stars in the sky. Sarah laughed at the promise of God since she was well past the child-bearing years, but God fulfilled his promise with the birth of Isaac. (You can read more about this story in Genesis chapters 16-21.)

Isaac, the son of Abraham and Sarah, married Rebekah. The Scriptures tell us in Genesis 25:21 that

Isaac pleaded to the Lord for his wife who was barren. It was 20 years after their marriage that the Lord blessed Isaac and Rebekah with twin sons, Jacob and Esau.

Jacob married sisters Rachel and Leah. Leah had six sons and a daughter, but the Lord had closed Rachel's womb. Rachel tried everything she could think of to have children. Once in anguish, she cried out to Jacob, "Give me children, or else I die" (Genesis 30:1). Jacob in anger replied, "Am I in God's stead, who hath withheld from thee the fruit of the womb?" It wasn't until the Lord opened her womb that she bore Joseph and Benjamin.

Elkanah had two wives. His favorite wife Hannah was barren. Peninnah, the other wife, taunted Hannah because she couldn't bear children during that particular time. Hannah pleaded with God to give her a son, promising to give him back to the Lord's work. God answered her prayer with the birth of Samuel, the last and greatest judge of Israel. (1 Samuel 1)

After God spoke words of promise into these women's lives, a new creature was created. That's for us today. If God has spoken over your life and you know the plans He has for you, all you need now is faith. Jeremiah 29:11 says, "For I know the thoughts that I think toward you, saith the Lord, thoughts of peace, and not of evil, to give you an expected end." My faith came when others doubted me. When I shared my dreams and visions with them, people said, "Yeah right." Then I decided to hold my piece and let God do the planning. He closed up every mouth that spoke evil against me. Of course "man" or people wouldn't believe that God can do such a thing for a sinner. Trust me, He will receive you as you are and forgive you of every sin you have ever committed.

    I can't imagine where my life would have ended if I didn't submit myself to the Lord. All things are possible with God. God knew exactly who I was going to become while I was going through my mess. He called me into purpose to be a successful business woman, wife, mother, and one of His leading ladies in the kingdom. Looking back over my life gives me hope for others. As a new creature in God, my past has allowed me to become a better servant to the Kingdom of God.

    After reading this chapter, if you feel that your life is barren, I would like to say this prayer to God on your behalf:

Lord,

I pray that Your will be done in the lives of Your people. I speak blessings over them in the name of the Lord Jesus Christ. If they are in a drought, I pray that you will pull them out right now. Lord, help them to shake the dust off their feet. Lord, forgive Your daughters of all wrong-doing. Be with them on their new journey. Let them know that the gifts they are carrying on the inside are ready to come forth. Help them give birth to their spiritual babies in the name of Jesus. Amen.

CHAPTER FIVE
Questions for Consideration

Has God given you a dream or prophetic word concerning His plans for you?

Are you in a season of doubt, doubting what God can do for you?

What do you believe God has predestined you to be, or has called you to do?

How can you break from the spirit of doubt? Encourage yourself and do the impossible.

Has anyone ever spoken against the plans that God has for you? Renounce those negative thoughts of the enemy in Jesus name.

Scriptures of Reflection

Acts 2:21 And it shall come to pass, [that] whosoever shall call on the name of the Lord shall be saved.

Philippians 3:14 - I press toward the mark for the prize of the high calling of God in Christ Jesus.

Psalms 37:4 - Delight thyself also in the LORD; and he shall give thee the desires of thine heart.

John 3:16 For God so loved the world, that he gave his only begotten Son, that whosoever believeth in him should not perish, but have everlasting life.

Luke 14:23 And the lord said unto the servant, Go out into the highways and hedges, and compel [them] to come in, that my house may be filled.

Mark 16:16 He that believeth and is baptized shall be saved; but he that believeth not shall be damned.

Mark 16:15 And he said unto them, Go ye into all the world, and preach the gospel to every creature.

CHAPTER SIX

From the Pit to the Palace

When you accept the call of God on your life, anything is possible. When I think of my life, I compare it to Joseph's life. As you know, Joseph was a dreamer. God gave Joseph big dreams, dreams of one day becoming a great ruler. One day, Joseph decided to share his dream with his family. After sharing his dreams with his brothers, they plotted to kill him.

The story of Joseph begins in Genesis 37:5-11: "And Joseph dreamed a dream, and he told it to his brethren; and they hated him yet the more. And he said unto them, "Hear, I pray you, this dream which I have dreamed: For, behold, we were binding sheaves in the field, and lo, my sheaf arose and also stood upright; and behold, your sheaves stood round about, and made obeisance to my sheaf."

And his brethren said to him, "Shalt thou indeed reign over us? Or shalt thou indeed have dominion over us?" And they hated him yet the more for his dreams and for his words.

And he dreamed yet another dream, and told it to his brethren and said, "Behold, I have dreamed one dream more; and behold, the sun and the moon and the eleven stars made obeisance to me."

And he told it to his father and to his brethren; and his father rebuked him and said unto him, "What is this dream that thou hast dreamed? Shall I and thy mother and thy brethren indeed come to bow down ourselves to thee to the earth?" And his brethren envied him, but his father observed the saying.

They may have tried to kill Joseph in his physical body, but they couldn't kill his destiny. Joseph was envied by his brothers. They couldn't understand the dream. "How shall he rein over us?" they thought. God had special plans for Joseph. Everything Joseph went through was for his position. He was thrown in a pit, lied on, and put in prison all for the glory of God. When we have problems with people, learn to look at them spiritually, not physically. People are not getting on your nerves just because it is what they want. Most of the time it's a spirit that is trying to attack you. If someone is constantly putting you down, or telling you that you can't accomplish something, then that's a dark force that is trying to hinder you from moving forward.

I like Joseph because he wasn't afraid of the trial. He stood his ground in every battle. God saw Joseph's determination and rewarded him for his perseverance. He was determined to bring his dream to pass. Many of you who are reading this book may feel like you are at the bottom. God has given you a dream that you are constantly trying to put to the side and it won't go away. That is a dream from God. It won't go away until you fulfill it. You have it in you to do whatever God has called you to do. God has given His children dominion throughout the earth. Our God has given us authority in the earth to call things into order.

I remember being at the bottom once, not having enough money to pay my bills or feeling like a failure, but not anymore. I am no longer dealing with many of the issues I dealt with earlier in life. I know how to handle them now. Dealing with frustration, confusion and anxiousness is no longer a part of my life. I am living my life stress-free. You can too!

Prayer is the key to your happiness. The old folks always said, "Don't worry about it, but pray about it". We sit and worry about things that are not important. Remove the unnecessary thoughts from your mind. Stop thinking about everybody else and think about yourself. There is nothing wrong with caring for yourself. We put so much emphasis on our children, our job, our family, and the issues of others and forget to care for ourselves. We forget the dreams we desire to fulfill. You can be a dreamer even after you have children. When we get married, we feel like our goals in life have to stop. No, they don't stop. They should be even better because you now have the support of your spouse. God wants to bless you with the desires of your heart. If you haven't accomplished two things you wanted to do in life, then now is the time. Get focused!

God is trying to bring some of us out of the pit, but we're too scared to give it all up for Him. It's like God is throwing the rope but we refuse to grab it. Stop worrying about who's going to agree or support you, the only support you need is from God. Leave everything else behind and move forward with your dreams. We want to hold on to old relationships. Let them go. If you are holding onto the father of your children who doesn't even desire to be with you, let him go. If you are keeping negative thoughts in your mind of what other people have said about you, let them go. It is time to drop off all the weight of your past. These are things that are keeping you from reaching your destiny. When you do this and seek the Lord for His will in your life, everything else will be added unto you. God is not the author of confusion. If your life is a wreck, yes, God can fix it. Once you decide to let your flesh die to the things of this world, there's no turning back. Destiny lies ahead waiting.

If God would have turned His back on me when I was out there in the world, I wouldn't be here today. I am a living testimony of a delivered soul from the pit. I was unclean, I was impure, I was unholy, but God still called me His child because He knew I was coming back to Him. I was His daughter. He knew me because He had already predestined who I was going to be before my mother gave birth to me. Just like God knew who I was when I was messed up, He knows you. You, as an individual, have to realize who you are in Christ. "Do not be conformed to this world, but be transformed by the renewing of your mind" Romans 12:2.

CHAPTER SIX
Questions for Consideration

Who are you?

Are you "putting off" living for God because you may feel unworthy?

Who, or what, is holding you from reaching your destiny?

What are you dreaming?

Are you hanging around dream-killers?

Scriptures of Reflection

3 John 1:2 Beloved, I wish above all things that thou mayest prosper and be in health, even as thy soul prospereth.

1 Corinthians 3:16 Know ye not that ye are the temple of God, and [that] the Spirit of God dwelleth in you?

Philippians 4:13 I can do all things through Christ which strengtheneth me.

Luke 10:27 And he answering said, Thou shalt love the Lord thy God with all thy heart, and with all thy soul, and with all thy strength, and with all thy mind; and thy neighbour as thyself.

CHAPTER SEVEN

You are Worthy

I chose to live because I desired a better future. If I would have chosen to stay in my present state, I would not have only died spiritually, but naturally as well. My daughter would have been without a mother. I probably would have ended up selling my body, or ended up with a life- threatening disease. I know women today who have caught some type of deadly disease and they are now living with a condition from which that "man" says is impossible to heal. To man, it might be impossible to eliminate, but God says our healing is in the palm of His hands.

People are dying daily. Women are having sex with strangers, or selling their bodies for cash, and using sex as a weapon to trap men. The spirit of lust is rampant. It is entering our children from television, movies, ads, school, and family members. This spirit has no respect for our children. Diseases are real and so are these spirits that are hovering over us, trying to make us perform unbiblical, sexual acts. This lifestyle will lead you to hell. I praise God for saving me. Can you imagine going to get a physical and receiving a phone call telling you to come in to the doctor's office, immediately? If we, as women, don't respect ourselves enough to wait on the Lord to send us His appointed spouse, you might one day receive a call from a doctor with unwelcoming news. God has given us power to overcome the spirit of sex and lust. Philippians 4:13 says, "I can do all things through Christ who strengthens me." Ladies, we can do it. We just need to get busy for God and declare that this freedom exists and it starts with us.

    I love the story of Ruth. Ruth was a poor, young, Moabite woman who later became a widow due to the death of her husband. Because of her loyalty to her mother-in-law, Naomi, she was taught and mentored by her to deal with various circumstances in life. After the death of Naomi's husband and sons, Ruth and Naomi traveled back to Bethlehem, Naomi's birthplace. Ruth was a hardworking young lady. She would go off in the fields to work, but on one particular day, she ran into the rich land owner, Boaz. What a blessing to be around someone like Naomi because she taught Ruth how to attract Boaz. Ruth and Boaz got married and had a son named Obed. Later on in the story, Ruth became the great-grandmother of King David (Ruth 1-4).

Just like Ruth, God has someone for you. You may feel like a widow, feeling lonely because you may have lost a mate or desiring to be loved again. God has a Boaz in the making just for you. I had to realize the same thing. Going on date after date, I was tired. Often getting hurt along the way, my feelings were getting tumbled over. Though the guys never treated me like rubbish, or unworthy, I felt unworthy. I wanted more than what they wanted. Like many women today, I was looking for love in the wrong places and for the wrong reasons. Throughout my course in life, I always felt a little left out. I think because of my loneliness, I tried to fill that void by dating. I didn't have a problem finding a boyfriend, just finding the perfect one for me. Mr. Boaz is in waiting, but the Lord also desires for you to be in the right position for when he brings Boaz to you.

Learning to love yourself is the most important step in being in a relationship with someone. If you don't love yourself, how can you love others? You deserve to feel loved and be loved. Don't settle for less. I don't care how your past relationship has ended; you have the right to be happy. Just because "Johnny" may have walked out and left you with kids, bills, car note, and loans to pay, that doesn't mean all men will do the same thing to you. I always admired my father. He always had a job. He worked twelve-hour shifts around the clock, providing for the family. Because I saw that at an early age, I desired to have that for my life. It is important that we be the first role model in our home. Children often desire to be what they see. Sometimes they may not want to be what they see, but because they are around it so much, it often becomes a part of their lives. If they see their mom with a different boyfriend every 3 months, they may pick up a thought that they are supposed to change their boyfriend every couple of months. If they see their father selling drugs, the idea of making quick money may seem interesting to them. These are the traits that we should not model for our children.

At a young age, I always knew I wanted to be married one day. Before the Lord sent my husband into my life, he had to heal me. You may wonder, "Healing from what?" I needed healing from past relationships, healing from the thought of unworthiness, healing from pain and trauma, healing from soul agreement with and acceptance of negative things in my life, and healing from the unknown. The Lord had to tear down the broken wall in order to add a new frame. All I could say is, "Lord work on me. I am a broken wreck and need to be fixed." I was all pretty on the outside and broken on the inside. You can try to hide the scars with all the make-up and accessories you can think of, but God is looking at your heart. He cares most about the inside. He wants His children to be bold and beautiful. Even with all the beautification we do on the outside, God desires us to be made whole on the inside. Whole meaning: healed completely in body, mind, soul, and spirit.

If you don't allow God to heal your body, mind, soul, and spirit, you will destroy every relationship you get into, not knowing why you can't keep a man. Your past can demolish your future. It's dangerous to walk around with the spirit of anger, bitterness, hatred, control, untrustworthiness, depression, isolation and rage. These are the spirits that will cause you to be in bondage. They will cause you to not forgive, love, or trust anyone. These spirits come to keep you lonely. If you are not careful, you may find yourself unknowingly walking under the spirit of Jezebel. This spirit easily attaches itself to us if we're not careful. This spirit wants to always be in control and is never satisfied.

Take the time to examine your relationship. Read each question and answer with an honest response.

Can you keep a boyfriend/girlfriend over 5 months?

Do people tend to be your friend, or run when they see you?

Do you hate everything about your mate?

Are you easy to please?

Are you always accusing your mate of cheating?

Are you always looking to find negative information on someone?

Do you have to snoop behind your mate to check his/her email, pockets, or car seeking to find something?

Do you always blame others for your problem or issues?

     If you have answered yes to any of these questions, you may need counseling or deliverance. If you're hurt, then you are liable to hurt others. God desires us to walk in peace, love, and a sound mind. He wants you to be free so that you can find love. Allow Him to bring healing to your emotions. You can't love others unless you love yourself. He wants you to trust and forgive. If you don't receive healing in your weak areas, then you can destroy the mate that God has prepared for you.

     Your mate wants to feel loved also. You can affect your relationship if you always feel like you can't trust anybody. People want to be in a peaceful relationship. If you're always accusing him, wanting to fight, putting him down with negatives words or controlling his life, he is going to get tired and leave you. I want to see each of you with the person

God has ordained for you. If you are still single, don't think that you can't find anyone or don't put your-self down, you may be in the preparation stage. God may be preparing your mate for you. You don't want someone who's messed up or not prepared. If you wait, I guarantee you that when he comes, he is going to be just right for you. Don't give into every man that you see. Keep yourself whole, saved and holy. Let your mate find you spotless.

Many women are not marrying their Boaz due to desperation. They are desperate and the devil knows it and is using it to his advantage. But on this day I claim you to be free. God has given you authority over the spirit of loneliness. You are loved. You are somebody. We have the greatest lover of life and His name is Jesus Christ. You don't have to look for love in all the wrong places because your heavenly Father loves you. John 15:13, "Greater love hath no man than this, that a man lay down his life for his friends".

If you are struggling right now in your flesh, I want to encourage you. Don't settle for less. Wait on your Boaz. Turn away from all unclean things. You can do it. You have the power to the break the bondage of sin in your family, over towns, cities and nations. Let's decree and declare that this generation will experience the God-kind of marriage and family unit, built on the same spiritual principals that have in biblical days brought peace, holiness, divine provision and prosperity to those who depended on God for their well-being. We can be the virgins that God has called us to be until Boaz asks our hand in marriage. Don't rush Boaz. Even though your Boaz was already created just for you, keep in mind that God will place you two together in His timing. God will have a set time for you to meet him, just be ready when that time comes!

CHAPTER SEVEN
Questions for Consideration

Did you do a self-examination?

What are your results?

Are you allowing God to make you whole?

Have you found your Boaz or is he still in the making?

What are you going to do to keep your mate?

What are you doing to keep your Boaz?

Scriptures of Reflection

Genesis 2:21-25 So the LORD God caused a deep sleep to fall upon the man, and while he slept took one of his ribs and closed up its place with flesh. And the rib that the LORD God had taken from the man he made into a woman and brought her to the man. Then the man said, "This at last is bone of my bones and flesh of my flesh; she shall be called Woman, because she was taken out of Man." Therefore a man shall leave his father and his mother and hold fast to his wife, and they shall become one flesh. And the man and his wife were both naked and were not ashamed.

Malachi 2:14, 15 But you say, "Why does he not?" Because the LORD was witness between you and the wife of your youth, to whom you have been faithless, though she is your companion and your wife by covenant.

1 Corinthians 7:2 But because of the temptation to sexual immorality, each man should have his own wife and each woman her own husband.

Hebrews 13:4 Let marriage be held in honor among all, and let the marriage bed be undefiled, for God will judge the sexually immoral and adulterous.

CHAPTER EIGHT

A Mother's Love

Many children desire to feel like they belong. I didn't have that special feeling when I was younger. I felt like I was different and couldn't find a place to fit in. Many of you may feel this way. So what do you do when you feel like you're the odd ball, the one that doesn't do what everybody else is doing, the one who sits back in the corner because they lack self-confidence or awareness? I was once that girl. Someone who felt lonely at times. Someone who often talked with God because I couldn't understand why I felt different. It wasn't about looking different, but there was something on the inside that caused me to ponder why I couldn't be a part of the so called "in" group.

There is a reason that God's people don't fit in with the world. We were born in the world, but we are not of the world. I had to eventually learn to set myself apart. I hung around some not-so-good people but, hey, I didn't care because I wanted to fit in. In my doing so, I ran into some road blocks that caused me lots of pain and grief at the end. I did some things in my life that I regret, but I know they're in the past. I can't change what happened, I only can learn from my mistakes.

There are some things in life as a parent we don't want our children to repeat. I have a long list of mistakes I've made, but I use them as an example for my children. I know they're not going to listen and do what they want to do, but my desire is to help them, coach them into the direction that will lead them into a path of success and not failure. After my first child, I could have chosen to sit back and live on welfare. I could have chosen to keep having more and more children because I knew the government would take care of them. Instead, I chose to opt out of the situation. I knew that "greater was He on the inside of me" and if I would have gotten stuck in that current state, I wouldn't have gone any further. I had to push my way out of some things, but thank God I made it.

You often may feel like God is pulling on you to let go of some things that He doesn't want you to be part of, but I encourage you to be obedient to His spirit. Sometimes we don't want to change our environment because we're too scared of what people are going to say or think. I've learned the hard way that regardless of what you do, people are going to talk about you anyway, so why not do the right thing? I felt trapped because I would always consider the feelings of others, but if I'm doing what God has called me to do, then why should I care? That makes sense right! Why care if people don't agree with what you're doing? If God is telling you what to do with your life, then why listen to those who are choosing to do things they desire that are not of God? You should not want to go to hell for anybody.

Decisions I made in life were sometimes not understandable to man, but in God's eyes it made total sense. When I got married, God directed me to move in with my husband who already had a home that was miles and miles away from my family. I left everything behind and didn't look back. I left wanting to leave the old behind, but there was always a pull on the inside for me to go back. So eventually, I started traveling back and forth ever so often, on the weekends, for a few months. I satisfied my flesh, but my spirit didn't agree. Things just weren't the same anymore. I finally realized that I had outgrown my past. The things I used to do weren't fun anymore, and the people I hung around, I saw them in a different way. My feelings changed. My desires changed. That's when I realized that God had my life going in a different direction than the people in my circle. Their lifestyle didn't line up with what He was doing in my life then, so He had to remove them. It wasn't because He doesn't love them. It was because I chose to surrender all of myself unto Him. Everything surrounding my life had to be about God. I had to give it all up. When I made that decision to do the right thing, not only for my life, but for my family, God began to move more in my life. I desired for things to be different for my daughters. Curses were broken because I chose to break the root by not living the way the devil desired for me to live.

If you love your children, let them see the God in you. Let your light shine so much that they will not depart from your guidance. Put down the alcohol, stop the foul language, keep them guarded from danger, pray over them daily and don't degrade them if they make a mistake, but encourage them to do the right thing the next time. Many children don't have a close bond with their parents. Today's parents are lacking communication and the showing of affection. We treat our children the way our parents treated us. When we got in trouble, we were called all kind of names. Let's do things differently this time. How about sitting them down to see what the problem is? They can be having problems at school, in the home, at church, or on the bus. We, as parents, don't find out what's going on because our normal routine is to whip them with the belt and find out later.

Our children are under attack. They are dealing with suicidal demons, emotional and behavioral problems, the spirit of depression, gender issues, drug usage, self-esteem, obesity, poverty, a lack of good role models, molestation, and so much more. Our children need us. We need to get ourselves together so that our children will have a better future. God didn't bless us with them to make money from them, but he allowed us to birth them so we can help replenish the earth with His children, for His glory. We have birthed doctors, lawyers, teachers, governors, but we can't see it. Just because some may have been born with a birth defect, or the doctor may have diagnosed them with a mental illness, don't give up on who God created them. Even in the midst of all the trouble it may take to raise a child, God is giving you the strength to do what He has called you to do. His desire is for us to be the best teachers to our children. We send our children to school for them to be taught by an educator with a degree, but the actual teaching begins at home.

I have taught students for many years and have also homeschooled my children, but I have never in my life seen so many children that lack respect for themselves, adults, and God. These children have missed some form of teaching along the way. We need to stand in the gap for the youth. It's not who has the most money, builds the biggest church, or drives the fanciest cars, God desires for us all to win our children back from society. They are not just a number in the system, but they are God-chosen vessels for His Kingdom. The devil would choose to sift them like wheat, but I know there is a Body of Believers that will raise up a standard against the enemy. It is time to tell the devil to back off of our seeds. You have it in you to be the best mother, father, aunt, uncle, and grandparent. It's time to show the children that we care.

CHAPTER EIGHT
Questions for Consideration

How can you be the best parent?

What are some things that you desire to change about yourself?

How do your children feel about you?

How can you change the outcome of your current relationship with your child?

Do plan to become a better role model for your family and others?

Scriptures of Reflection

Ephesians 6:4 - And, ye fathers, provoke not your children to wrath: but bring them up in the nurture and admonition of the Lord.

Proverbs 22:6 - Train up a child in the way he should go: and when he is old, he will not depart from it.

Colossians 3:21 - Fathers, provoke not your children [to anger], lest they be discouraged.

Ephesians 6:1 - 6:4 Children, obey your parents in the Lord: for this is right. Honour thy father and mother; (which is the first commandment with promise ;) That it may be well with thee, and thou mayest live long on the earth.

CHAPTER NINE

Keep Your Vision Alive

So David rose early in the morning, left the sheep with a keeper, and took the things and went as Jesse had commanded him. And he came to the camp as the army was going out to the fight and shouting for the battle. For Israel and the Philistines had drawn up in battle array, army against army. And David left his supplies in the hand of the supply keeper, ran to the army, and came and greeted his brothers. Then as he talked with them, there was the champion, the Philistine of Gath, Goliath by name, coming up from the armies of the Philistines; and he spoke according to the same words. So David heard them. And all the men of Israel, when they saw the man, fled from

him and were dreadfully afraid. So the men of Israel said, "Have you seen this man who has come up? Surely he has come up to defy Israel; and it shall be that the man who kills him the king will enrich with great riches, will give him his daughter, and give his father's house exemption from taxes in Israel." (1 Samuel 17:20-25)

When you read the story in the Bible about David and Goliath, does your mind begins to form a vivid picture of the account? The Bible is a book that we believe in. We weren't living in Biblical times so we have to believe and picture in our mind what took place in the Bible years ago. When we look at this particular story of David and Goliath, based on our natural thinking, it's hard to believe that a teenager could defeat a giant that stood over 9 feet tall.

When David went against Goliath, he used three things:

Vision
Faith
Belief

David was successful because he imagined himself winning the battle. He said, "If I can kill a bear and lion, then I can kill a giant." He had a vision. Many of us are facing giants in our life and we are too afraid to fight, but I hear the Lord say, "No weapon formed against you shall prosper." David had faith. For the Bible says in Matthew 17:20 "...If ye have faith as a grain of mustard seed, ye shall say unto this mountain, Remove hence to yonder place; and it shall remove; and nothing shall be impossible unto you." David had faith in God. He approached the giant with five stones but only used one.

When you have faith, you also have to believe. David imagined it, had faith in God, then he believed in himself to do the impossible. Many of us don't know how big our God is. Our God is the creator of the universe. He made the stars, the moon, the light, the plants, the animals, Adam, Eve, and placed Jesus in Mary's womb. If we claim to be His children, then we need to begin to think the impossible. That's why Romans 12:2 tells us to renew our mind. If we always think small then we're going to have small outcomes. David thought big so the outcome of his battle was great. It was beyond great, it was victorious. It was on a whole new level. Proverbs 29:18 says, "Where there is no vision, the people perish." Vision is the state of seeing with your eyes. It is the act or power of anticipating that which will be. It is important to have a vision. Without vision, your life will be dull, dry, and dead. There are many people walking around today with no vision. They wake up to follow the same routine for weeks, months and years at a time. I cannot repeat last year's cycle. I'm ready for the new vision. Next year has to be greater. I am tired of dealing with the same people, the same demons, and the same work schedule. Something has to change. Women, you have to desire a change for your life.

In all seriousness, the Lord wants to bless you. He doesn't want to withhold things from you, but He wants to give to you. He wants to hand out some blessings. He wants to give you joy. He wants to give you peace. He wants to give you hope. He wants to give you love. He wants to give you faith. He wants you to experience salvation. He wants to heal your pain and He wants to bring you freedom. God desires to give you all that your heart desires, but you have to be in a positive position to receive.

We cannot receive from God with a closed mind and a closed fist. God wants us in a ready position. He's the quarter back trying to throw us a blessing but we, the receivers, are looking the other way. We need to look in the right direction this season. We need to be looking for the miracles, looking for the blessings, looking for the breakthroughs and looking for the healings. We need to stop walking around with our head down. Learn to hold your head up and look up because that is where our help and strength comes from.

Let this year be different for you. When I made my mind up to get right with God, I told the Lord, I'm ready for a new dimension in Him. The Lord desires to make you new. He wants to renew your mind. He wants to change your heart. He wants to make you whole. And the only way to be whole is to totally be submitted unto Him. After you submit yourselves, allow Him to bring your life into alignment and order. He wants to rearrange your life from mess to success. He needs to take away the old and put in the new. You should be in a season with new thinking; thinking the impossible, replacing the "I can't" with "I can."

Don't abort your dreams. For the Bible says, "sing, Oh, barren!" Somebody who is reading this book is about to produce their vision. God is about to enlarge your territory. Don't let the devil tell you that you can't do it, because you can. You can be that doctor. You can be that lawyer. You can be that actor or singer. You can be a teacher, or that leader. You can be that godly wife or husband. You can walk in holiness, you can walk in love, you can walk in peace. Psalms 37:4 - Delight thyself also in the LORD; and he shall give thee the desires of thine heart. Everyone has talents and abilities that when developed will make them prosperous in life. You are a successful individual. God has anointed your hands to do great things.

There were many women in the Bible who were barren, but the Lord touched their wombs and brought forth a child. Your barren days are over. I speak to the wombs of God's children and command the visions to live.

This is the year. This is the year to see changes. This is the year of supernatural blessings. Your next year is the year of double blessings. God wants to open the floodgates and pour out blessings on His people. Daniel 10:7 "And I, Daniel, alone saw the vision, for the men with me did not see the vision." In this season, God is going to open some eyes to the supernatural. God will show you but not others.

God didn't turn His back on you, but He kept you and me because He has predestined us to greatness. You don't have to live in poverty, lack, or shortage. We often feel like Elijah in the book of 1 Kings 16. Elijah went through a season of drought, but his hope in God was bigger than his natural mind. He didn't give up, but he stayed on the course. Let's take a look at Elijah's story. Elijah, the prophet, whose life was lived in the presence of God, stood before Ahab the King of Israel to predict a three-year drought because of the King's sins and the sins of the people. When the famine came, Elijah was told by God to head near the brook of Cherith, a small stream of the Jordan River. Here, in this lonely place, Elijah was well taken care of by the divine care of God. God sent the ravens to Elijah every single day to bring him food while the running brook furnished him with water. While the land throughout Israel was dried up and deserted from the famine, Elijah stayed by the brook in the comfort that God provided for him. But then came the day when the stream of water stopped flowing. Elijah stooped to drink, but there was no water. The brook had dried up. Elijah's resources were no longer available. There was no sound of running water, no whisper of the wind, and no tweeting of the birds.

Now life can often be like that. We have all ran into a season of drought, emptiness, defeat and loss. A time when it seems that life has died, hope has died, faith has died, dreams have died, and you no longer want to go on.

Sometimes in our lives, we have to go through a season of dryness. I don't know about you but that is the toughest season to go through. The feeling of not having, borrowing, begging, pleading, and financing just to get through. I thank God for layaway plans. Even when we're broke, God allows us to put what we desire on layaway. We love layaways so much, some of us have even put our praise on layaway. But God says get your praise off of layaway and start praising Him now for your harvest. We need to learn to praise God for the vision. There are some things you desire right now. Start praising God for the things you don't have but you know that are on the way. God is looking for people to praise Him in the midst of only having little. God can turn that little into a lot in a matter of seconds.

We are so used to having everything we need so that when that season of dryness comes, we go into panic mode. Instead of trusting God, we get frustrated. We begin to worry...Lord, how am I going pay this or pay that? How am I going to do this or complete that? But it is only a test. Elijah made it through the drought because he had faith in God.

Sometimes God will put your faith to the test. Hebrews 11:1 "Now faith is the substance of things hoped for, the evidence of things not seen." Faith is believing in the unseen. Sometimes when you're going through, you may not see your way out but you've got to believe that you're coming out. Tell yourself, "I'm coming out of this one." When God told Noah to build the ark, he built it by faith. God was preparing Noah for the things to come, but it took Noah's faith and obedience to act upon the instructions. Noah could have said, "Well God, I will build the ark when I see the rain", but if he would have waited, he and his family would have never survived the flood. So faith is not what you see, but it's about believing that something will happen if God said it's going to happen.

There are times we need to stop asking God so many questions and just do what He tells us to do. You cannot make it in this life without faith. You have to live a life knowing that all things are possible if you believe in Jesus Christ. Elijah knew he was going to survive the drought. Daniel knew he was coming out of the lion's den. Joseph knew he was coming out of the pit. Joshua knew he was going to win the battle. Job knew his faith was going to be tested. All of them knew they were going to survive because they had faith in God. Do you have faith in God?

Do you have faith that God is going to pay your car note? Do you have faith that God is going to pay your mortgage or your rent? Do you have faith that God has your job secured? Do you have faith to know you shall never go a day without food? If you don't know this, then you should know, because it is written in His word, that He is going to supply all of your needs.

Every time God gave Elijah an instruction...he obeyed. We are living in a season now where faith and obedience need to work together. Elijah wouldn't have been able to save the widow's son if he didn't have faith in God. After the brook dried up and the ravens stopped coming, God told Eli-jah to go to Zarephath. Elijah didn't know what was going to happen in Zarephath, but he obeyed God. And by his obedience he was fed in the drought and was able to be used by God to raise the women's son from the dead.

When we look at Elijah's story, God gave Elijah specific instructions and he immediately reacted. He didn't wait or question God, but he did what God told him to do. First, God told him to tell Ahab that God was going to cut off his water supply. Then, God directed Elijah to go to Cherith to drink from the brook. So Elijah did as God commanded and was able to drink when the King and his Baal worshippers were in their season of drought. Listen to the revelation in that statement. Elijah had something to drink even though there was a drought in the land. When you are in a season of drought, remember the Word of the Lord. (Philippians 4:19) But my God shall supply all your need according to his riches in glory by Christ Jesus. Just because your neighbor is in a drought, it doesn't mean that it is your season of drought. You can live in the same house and still experience different seasons of drought. Your season of drought depends on your faith. God is trying to get His people in a position where we can only depend on God. Elijah was able to survive the season of drought because of his obedience and his faith in God. In the meanwhile, Elijah was being tested while God was preparing him for his next challenge.

God never said this walk was going to be easy, but He said you shall have life, and have it more abundantly. When you are going through, only know that it is for a season. The pain that you are facing now is preparing you for your greater good. As women, some of us feel like we have to suffer for nine months when we're pregnant, but look at the greater result after the pain. The pain and the suffering can be worth it. God was preparing Elijah for the battle. He was refining Elijah for the opposition he had to face against the prophets of Baal. God won't send you through a storm unless he knows you are prepared for it. Elijah was able to prove he was a real prophet of God because he knew his faith in the Lord was strong. He was able to challenge the men to a battle and won because he knew his God wasn't going to fail him.

How strong is your faith today? Do you believe that you're coming out of your drought? Do you believe that your vision for your life will come to pass? God has a plan for your life. I, often at times, thought that I would have never made it past three years in my marriage. I often felt that I would never complete this book, which was prophesied over four years ago. I never thought I would be pastoring a church. By the grace of God, these goals have been achieved and accomplished because I stood on the Word of God. I didn't look at what I didn't have, but I looked at the things that God has provided for me: a supporting husband, the will to do, and the faith and mind to react.

Just like God gave Elijah instructions, he has been doing the same to you. Are you listening to His voice? Are you being obedient to His directions? You are a child of God. There is no way that He will leave you without instructions. When He speaks:

listen, obey and react. You have visions, dreams and destiny in you. Live them out. Fulfill the void in your life by completing your goals. Don't let your vision die, but keep it alive by doing the work. You are talented with great potential. Believe in yourself. Get started by asking God to repeat the directions and be led by the Holy Spirit on your next move. I am looking forward to seeing and reading the success of my readers. It's in you. Let it flow from your spirit. God is waiting for you to take a step forward and He will do the rest.

CHAPTER NINE
Questions for Consideration

What is it that you want to do?

What process or measure have you started to take?

What are some tools or resources you have available to start?

What are you led in spirit to do at this present moment?

Scriptures of Reflection

Decree and Declare these scriptures over your life:

I am loved. 1 John 3:3

I am accepted. Ephesians 1:6

I am a child of God. John 1:12

I am Jesus' friend. John 15:14

I am a joint heir of Jesus. Romans 8:17

I am free from sin. Romans 8:1

I am a new creature. 2 Corinthians 5:17

I am anointed. 2 Corinthians 1:21

I am seated in heavenly places with Christ. Ephesians 2:6

I have direct access to God. Ephesians 2:18

I am chosen to bear fruit. John 15:16

I am a temple of God. 1 Corinthians 6:19

I am a member of Christ's body. 1 Corinthians 12:27

I am a Saint. Ephesians 1:1

I am forgiven. Colossians 1:14

I am complete in Jesus Christ. Colossians 2:10

CHAPTER TEN

This is Your Season

You may be reading this book, feeling as if there is no hope for your situation. There is hope.

We all know this familiar story. Lazarus, the brother of Mary and Martha, and friend of Jesus, had died. The Bible says that He was placed in a cave which was covered with a stone. If you can, picture in your mind a lifeless man. When you think of the term 'dead', you think of the words departed or deceased...something that will never be put back together again. But here, in this story, Jesus said that Lazarus' death was only temporary. Lazarus had to experience this physical death so that the Son of God may be glorified.

    We sometimes need to be reminded that the great "I AM" is here even in the midst of our trials and tribulations. Notice, Jesus calls him by name. Jesus knew exactly who He wanted to come forth. He doesn't just announce a general calling by saying, "Come forth", where a bunch of graves could open up and there'd be all these resurrected bodies standing there. He announced that Lazarus should come forth. His call to Lazarus was personal, precise, and powerful. When God calls you, He's calling life, He's calling the healing, He's calling the breakthroughs, He's calling deliverance, He's calling miracles, and He's calling the finances. Your name is being called, just like Lazarus. There is a purpose for your coming forth.

    Remember, Tabitha, in the book of Acts, known as Dorcas, was sick and died. The Bible said that Peter knelt down and prayed and said to the body, "Tabitha, arise", and she open her eyes and sat up. Tabitha couldn't die because the people in her town needed her. Then there's Jairus' daughter. The Bible says in Mark 5, as Jesus was crossing over to the other side of the sea, He was approached by a ruler name Jairus. Jairus told Jesus that his little girl was to the point of death. So Jesus pressed His way through the crowd to get to Jairus' house, but by the time He arrived, she was already dead. Jesus then told the crowd that the little was sleeping and went into room where she laid and said, "little girl arise".

When God calls you, you better believe that He's calling things into alignment in your life. God wants to encourage every reader. God says that your current situation is only temporary. What may look physically impossible to us is possible through our Lord and Savior Jesus Christ. Everything happens according to the will of God. God had to remind Martha that He is the resurrection and the life. Then He says, "He who believes in Me, though he may die, he shall live. And whoever lives and believes in Me shall never die" (John 11:25-26). Jesus is the light, He is the way, He is the truth, and He is the security.

Even though Lazarus was dead, Jesus had to show the Jews that He is God...He said, "I am going to raise him up, resurrect his life, and give Him life." Why? That God may be glorified. This is someone's story today, your business may be dead, your finances may be dead, your marriage may be dead, your career may look dead, but on this day, I leave you with this...it's not dead, it's only sleeping that God may get the glory out of your situation. Praise God that His resurrection power is at work in you.

God's power is in you. You can do the impossible. You can think the impossible. You can live the impossible life you desire. Whatever God has put in you must come out of you. That desire, that just won't go away, can flourish. Discipline yourself enough to begin to put that thought on paper and work out a plan.

I've always had the desire to be married, to be an entrepreneur, to be a teacher and to be a writer. I had to believe in myself first. When you feel useless, you have a lack of confidence in yourself. When you are rejected, you feel nothing good will ever happen for you. Those are all tricks of the enemy. Find, in your spirit, what exactly you want to do and start planning. Many people are blessed to have doors open because of the people they are connected to. Others have to put a foot forward and begin to work. You have to start somewhere. Don't just watch others around you, motivate yourself to activate your faith.

CHAPTER TEN
Questions for Consideration

What do you feel led to do at this time?

How soon are you ready to start achieving your goal?

How do you plan to begin this new journey?

Who can help you?

Scriptures of Reflection

Colossians 3:23 - And whatsoever ye do, do [it] heartily, as to the Lord, and not unto men;

2 Thessalonians 3:10 - For even when we were with you, this we commanded you, that if any would not work, neither should he eat.

Proverbs 14:23 - In all labour there is profit: but the talk of the lips [tendeth] only to penury.

Ecclesiastes 9:10 - Whatsoever thy hand findeth to do, do [it] with thy might; for [there is] no work, nor device, nor knowledge, nor wisdom, in the grave, whither thou goest.

Acts 20:35 - I have shewed you all things, how that so labouring ye ought to support the weak, and to remember the words of the Lord Jesus, how he said, It is more blessed to give than to receive.

Proverbs 12:11 - He that tilleth his land shall be satisfied with bread: but he that followeth vain [persons is] void of understanding.

Proverbs 10:4 - He becometh poor that dealeth [with] a slack hand: but the hand of the diligent maketh rich.

Proverbs 21:25 - The desire of the slothful killeth him; for his hands refuse to labour.

CHAPTER ELEVEN

The Anointing

There were many times I got crossed up in the flame of the fire, being in the wrong places at the wrong time. I could've gotten shot, beaten up, or killed, but because of the anointing of the Holy Spirit, I am still standing. If it wasn't for the grace of God, the devil would have taken me out of here years ago. Thanks be to God that He saw fit that I would live to do the work of the Lord. The same anointing that covered me is covering you. God sent His power and the Holy Spirit to earth to save us, to deliver us, and to guide us. You may not know about this anointing, but the anointing and power that you are walking in is the only reason you are still living.

You have the anointing to forgive yourself of your own sins. I could have given up a long time ago because of what I did in my past. We are told to forgive others when they trespass against us and seek forgiveness. When we ask God for forgiveness, He forgives us. We are forgiven once we have believed that He died on the cross and we trust Him as our Lord and Savior. It is just that simple. However, many have been released from the bondage of sin (as spoken of in Romans chapters 6-8), but still choose to stumble in it and act as though we are not freed from sin. Likewise, with the guilty feelings that we feel, we can choose to accept the fact that we are forgiven in Christ, or we can believe the devil's lie that we are still guilty and should, therefore, feel guilty.

When God forgives you, He will not bring up your past. The Bible tells us that He will remember our sins no more. You can move from your bondage state and into the anointing that God has placed on your life. Use your past as a testimony of where God has delivered you from and compare it to the place He is taking you.

The anointing allowed me to move on from my mistakes. Forget about the sins you have committed. Forgive those who have hurt or offended you. Walk away from the backstabbers. Look away from the hypocrites. Anything that is hindering you from moving forward, God is commanding you to walk away from the bondages in your life.

You have the anointing of God flowing through you. The anointing of God is the Holy Spirit. He flows as a river of love, from the throne of grace, through the hearts of believers, bringing life to all who receive His touch.

God anoints people that love Him more than they love their own lives. As we open our hearts to love others more than God, God will allow His anointing to stop flowing. When we close our hearts and become cold-hearted, we grieve the Holy Spirit. You don't want the Holy Spirit to leave you. We need the anointing to live. We need the anointing to survive. We need the anointing to prosper.

Because of the anointing we are able to:

1. to preach the Gospel to the poor
2. to heal and restore people by faith
3. to proclaim freedom to the captives
4. to open blind eyes by faith
5. to set people free
6. operate in God's timing

I survive daily because of who lives on the inside of me. I was able to bounce back from my failures. The power of the anointing allowed me to be around the sins that once had me bound, but it also gave me the victory to not give in to them.

Don't quench the Holy Spirit which lives on the inside of you. You have the power to win over every weak spot in your life.

    I survived because I chose to walk with the Lord. When I surrendered my life unto Him, I allowed the Holy Spirit to come into my life in a greater way. You are powerful. You have purpose. Don't take life for granted and get right with God. If you desire to get in a better position with God, say the prayer below and be free in Jesus name!

Prayer

Lord, I come to You in the name of Jesus, asking You to forgive of all my sins. I open my heart to receive You. Jesus, You are my Lord and Savior. I know You died for my sins and You have risen from the dead. Lord Jesus, fill me with your Holy Spirit. I thank You Father for saving me in Jesus' name. Amen.

"For whoever shall call upon the name of the Lord shall be saved." Romans 10:13

CHAPTER ELEVEN
Questions for Consideration

What do you feel God is leading you to walk away from?

How do you plan to forgive yourself?

Are you willing to walk in the anointing and power that God has given you?

Are you willing to surrender your all to Him today?

Scriptures of Reflection

1 John 2:27 But the anointing which ye have received of him abideth in you, and ye need not that any man teach you: but as the same anointing teacheth you of all things, and is truth, and is no lie, and even as it hath taught you, ye shall abide in him.

Luke 4:18 The Spirit of the Lord [is] upon me, because he hath anointed me to preach the gospel to the poor; he hath sent me to heal the brokenhearted, to preach deliverance to the captives, and recovering of sight to the blind, to set at liberty them that are bruised...

James 5:14 Is any sick among you? Let him call for the elders of the church; and let them pray over him, anointing him with oil in the name of the Lord:

1 Samuel 16:13 Then Samuel took the horn of oil, and anointed him in the midst of his brethren: and the Spirit of the LORD came upon David from that day forward. So Samuel rose up, and went to Ramah.

Isaiah 10:27 And it shall come to pass in that day, [that] his burden shall be taken away from off thy shoulder, and his yoke from off thy neck, and the yoke shall be destroyed because of the anointing.

CHAPTER TWELVE

For Pastor's Wives Only

You were called by God to use your own unique gift. When you realize what gift(s) God has placed on the inside of you, will feel more confident in the ministry where He has called you. In the New Testament, you will find many women in the Bible that God used in different measure, in their time:

Philip's daughters: "prophesied" (Acts 21:9)

Phoebe: "a servant of the church" (Rom. 16:1)

Widows: serving and interceding (1 Tim. 5:3-10)

Anna: "prophetess ... fasting and praying" (Luke 2:36-37)

Dorcas: "doing good and helping the poor" (Acts 9:36)

Lydia: showing hospitality (Acts 16:15)

Priscilla: teaching "the way of God" (Acts 18:26)

God has given each one of His children spiritual gifts which correspond to their personality and calling which, in return, will be used to fulfill their duties so they can be more effective in ministry, as well as in life, in accordance with their gifts. Seek God concerning your role in your family, church, and community. You are important to the church, as well as your spouse. He will need you more than you think. When he's down, you will be there to lift him up. Don't ever feel that you are not anointed enough to be an aid to your husband. God called you to be his wife, partner and friend.

As a pastor's wife, we must understand that our lives are normal. We will experience everyday challenges and struggles. We have up days, and then we will have some down days. The difference from everyone else depends on how we handle our bad days. As leaders, one of our goals is to model how God would desire for us to handle certain situations. People may get on our nerves, curse us out, gossip, and slander our names, but God tells us in

Ecclesiastes 5:2 (KJV) 2 Be not rash with thy mouth, and let not thine heart be hasty to utter anything before God: for God is in heaven, and thou upon earth: therefore let thy words be few. We are to handle these types of situations with the direction of the Holy Spirit. We are not to take our anger out on social media, in the pulpit, or by violent altercation. So many things have happened to me in ministry, but by the grace of God, I didn't break. My name and character were slandered. I was lied on and talked about, but I refused to give in to the trick of the enemy. I refused to allow the spirit of depression to take a hold of my life. I encourage you, woman of God, to stand firm against all adversaries. There will be a lot of weight riding on your shoulders, but God will not put any more on us then we can bear.

Remember, you will be your husband's #1 supporter. You will witness the behind-the-door pain that leaders go through. Your husband will need your help as he will certainly go through persecution. He may go through false accusations, slandering of his name, and false rumors, but your job is to stand by your husband. During these trying times of ministry, you must support him in whatever capacity he needs you. He may be able to tell you some things that he can tell no other person. It is important that you and your spouse have clear communication and trust in your relationship. You both will need to be each other's backbone and support system. Only you can be the best mother and wife to your family.

Next, be original. Be yourself, God did not make any person the same and we were all born with uniqueness. You will be compared to other pastors' wives or to other female leaders. Don't get pushed into that corner. Allow Him to shape and mold you the way He desires. I had to change a lot of things about myself along the way. I learned that the person I was before ministry was not the person God created. I wasn't true to myself. I was uncomfortable with the person I became along the way by allowing people to attach themselves to me who didn't belong. I began to take on the traits of others. I did things that I can't take back, but what I do know is that God has forgiven me of my past sin and I solemnly choose not to return that way again. I may not have always been the perfect angel in life, but God has cleaned me up to become that virtuous woman He created me to be.

You don't need to be jealous or envious of any other female. Life is not about how many degrees one holds or how many accolades are behind your name. God is looking for willing vessels that desire to be used for His glory. Everything that God has given you is enough for you to take care of your household and ministry. You do not have to fear anyone taking your position as your husband's wife because you were called to be his helpmeet. The two of you will have such a bond that no man can separate. There will be times that he will need to call on outside assistance to help with the load he is carrying. God will place people in both your lives to be of help to the two of you, because ministry is not a one man's job. You will be able to help in ways that no other can help. Then there will be others that are assigned to you both to aid you in ministry. Your position as his wife is to cover him in prayer at all times. When you're going through, you will need an outlet as well. Find that prayer partner who can carry the two of you in prayer. Make sure it's someone that you can trust to share personal information. Your personal information is very valuable. Remember, anything you share openly can never be returned.

As women, we have a major role in society. We are not only mothers to our biological children, but we are remodels for others. Titus 2 (KJV) says, "But speak thou the things which become sound doctrine: 2 That the aged men be sober, grave, temperate, sound in faith, in charity, in patience.3 The aged women likewise, that they be in behaviour as becometh holiness, not false accusers, not given to much wine, teachers of good things; 4 That they may teach the young women to be sober, to love their husbands, to love their children...". We are to model godly behavior, character, and appearance at all times. If we have been delivered from the world, then we need to show that the world no longer has control over us. We are to guide the people of God into true holiness and sanctification. This generation is seeking help from the church. Many are stuck in chains and bondages but desire to be free. I can help, and you can help. Let's start by showing them the godly love that they are yearning for. Help point them towards Christ because He is the only way to true salvation.

I share my testimony as God leads me. There are so many hurting women in the Body of Christ because we chose to hide our pain, wondering how people may view us after they find out what is really in our closet. As we examine our life and tell the real story, they too would admit that their story is similar to ours. I can talk about my story because it used be a story, but it is now a testimony. A testimony means that I have already went through the struggle and now I can brag about how good my God is. He kept me from getting caught in a drug raid, hid me from a bullet, and kept me from the diseases of sin. Remember, no one is perfect. The God that changed my life will change yours, and the next person, and the next. He is the author and finisher of our life. He knew the beginning before the beginning even started, and He knows how it is going to end.

You may be a pastor's wife, dating a minister, or a woman in ministry. On this day, I ask you to take a look at your life. If there is anything that you are dealing with silently, I ask that you give it to

God. He already knows about it, but is just waiting for you to give it to Him. Don't walk around with a heavy heart. Allow God to heal any burden you may be carrying from church hurt, your past, or any abuse. You may have inner struggles from your past that desire to come back (jealousy, anger, strife, controlling, past hurt, etc.), I would strongly encourage you to seek spiritual guidance to help you deal with any problems you may have. There is nothing to be embarrassed about, just pray to God about any weakness in your life and seek deliverance or help. This will really help you along the way!

    I wrote this book to help women in all walks of life. God allowed us to experience things in life so that we can one day help and nurture others. People look at my life and think that I was always this way: brilliant, beautiful on the inside and out, with no flaws, not knowing that I once sat in the same seat they may be sitting in. The difference is, I gave up that seat for something greater when I died to the flesh and totally surrendered myself to Christ. As a pastor's wife, or woman in ministry, all eyes will be on you. Be the woman God called you to be. Walk in boldness and holiness. Live a lifestyle that will be pleasing unto God. You always feel like you have to please the people. I encourage you to live for Christ, then you can live for others.

CHAPTER TWELVE
Questions for Consideration

How are you willing to become a better wife and mother?

What are some things you are willing to change in your marriage to make it better for your spouse?

What would you like to give or support more in the ministry?

Are you being the best role model for God's people?

Are you setting a godly example for yourself, children, church and the community?
Are you showing modesty and godliness in your everyday walk with Christ?

Scriptures of Reflection

Proverbs 12:4 - A virtuous woman [is] a crown to her husband: but she that maketh ashamed [is] as rottenness in his bones.

Psalms 68:6 - God setteth the solitary in families: he bringeth out those which are bound with chains: but the rebellious dwell in a dry [land].

Ruth 3:11 - And now, my daughter, fear not; I will do to thee all that thou requirest: for all the city of my people doth know that thou [art] a virtuous woman.

2 Peter 1:3 - According as his divine power hath given unto us all things that [pertain] unto life and godliness, through the knowledge of him that hath called us to glory and virtue:

1 Peter 3:7 - Likewise, ye husbands, dwell with [them] according to knowledge, giving honour unto the wife, as unto the weaker vessel, and as being heirs together of the grace of life; that your prayers be not hindered.

Titus 2:5 - [To be] discreet, chaste, keepers at home, good, obedient to their own husbands, that the word of God be not blasphemed.

Dear Reader,

    I pray that you were blessed from my testimony. This is only the beginning. God has so much more in store for you and I. Everybody has a testimony. You too have a testimony. Allow your testimony to push you into greatness. Don't die in your situation but rise. Rise to the top of your generation and family. I speak power into your life that you may be empowered to fulfill your God given purpose for your life. It's never too late for God. If you are backslidden and feel like God has left you, He hasn't. He's still with you. Repeat this prayer of salvation and be free on today.

Prayer of Salvation

Lord, I come to you in the name of Jesus. I acknowledge that I am a sinner, and I am sorry for my sins and the life that I once lived; I ask for forgiveness. I believe that your son, Jesus Christ died for my sins, was resurrected from the dead, is alive, and hears my prayer. On this day, I invite Jesus to become the Lord of my life, to rule and reign in my heart from this day forward and forever more. You said in Your Holy Word, Romans 10:9, that if we confess the Lord our God and believe in our hearts that God raised Jesus from the dead, we shall be saved. Lord, send your Holy Spirit to help me obey You, and to do Your will for the rest of my life. In Jesus' name I pray, Amen.

About the Author

Jennifer Clark serves diligently as Elect Lady and Senior Director of the Women's Ministry at Global Outreach Ministries of Columbia, S.C.

At the heart of her ministry is her passion for issues relating to marriage, parenting, women in leadership, and pastors' wives functioning within their God-given call to help their husbands.

One of Jennifer's desires is to see women come to the knowledge of who they are in Christ. This has compelled her to establish The Elected Women's Ministry. The Elected Women's Ministry is an outreach program designed to help women redirect their steps and be empowered to return to their rightful place as ladies, nurturers, mothers, and wives.

Jennifer is also the mother of two beautiful daughters, an entrepreneur, and author. The success of her balanced life is attributed to her wisdom through prayer, fasting, and perseverance.

For speaking engagements, lectures or interviews, feel free to contact:

Jennifer Clark
Email: jclarkcompany@gmail.com

Additional copies of this book can be purchased from Rain Publishing and online bookstores.

Send a request to:

Please include the following with your order: Title, number of copies, shipping address, contact information, payment ($12.99 x # of copies), including shipping ($5.00), and mail to:

Jennifer Clark/Rain Publishing
PO Box 702
Knightdale, NC 27545

www.ingramcontent.com/pod-product-compliance
Lightning Source LLC
Chambersburg PA
CBHW071927290426
44110CB00013B/1506